Price Guide

Holt-Howard Collectibles

And Related Ceramicwares of the '50s & '60s

Walter Dworkin

Published by

krause
publications

700 E. State Street • Iola, WI 54990-0001

Please, call or write us for our free catalog of antiques and collectibles publications.
To place an order or receive our free catalog, call 800-258-0929.
For editorial comment and further information, use our regular business telephone at (715) 445-2214.

Library of Congress Catalog Number: 97-80622
ISBN: 0-87341-517-5
Printed in the United States of America

This book is dedicated to Randy Vaccaro, a true friend and companion who really knows the meaning of giving and without whose support and help, this book would never have been possible.

Also to Florence and Bernard Dworkin, two wonderful loving parents whose lifelong support and caring have always meant the world to me.

TABLE OF CONTENTS

take a peek

Welcome to a world of novelty ceramic collectibles from yesteryear. The time was the late 1950s through early 1960s when so many of our favorite collectibles were being manufactured in and imported from Japan. This era has become a very nostalgic time for us in the United States, always reminding us of past holidays and times gone by. Although this era is gone forever, it has left us with a treasure-trove of wonderful novelty collectibles to seek out, purchase, display and enjoy.

For Baby Boomers who grew up in the late 1950s, it was a wonderful period of creativity and transition. Rock 'n Roll was born, which turned our country upside-down. Beautifully designed streamlined cars with large tail fins that looked like rocket ships were invading our highways. Danish modern furniture was the home-decorating rage, pushing almost all of grandma's antiques out the front door. It was a time of Dick Clark's "American Bandstand," sock hops, poodle skirts, bobby socks and greasy D.A. hair-dos. The "I Love Lucy Show" took America by storm, and Marilyn Monroe and James Dean had risen to movie-idol status.

The 1950s was also a time of expansion. New homes were cropping up everywhere, affording people the luxury of space (both indoors and out). As a result, many families now had full-size kitchens, dinning rooms and dens to display their cherished belongings and collectibles. Best of all, barbecue grills were popping up everywhere, which created a market for condiment jars of all kinds. Americans now needed portable containers and jars to transport condiments and other goodies outdoors to picnic tables and grill areas.

During the late 1950s, with almost perfect timing, a most creative and clever company named Holt-Howard was developing a revolutionary new concept in deep-glazed ceramics called "Pixiewares." These containers included covered condiment jars featuring whimsical pixie heads perched on the top.

Due to the huge success of Pixiewares, other novelty companies such as Davar, Lefton, Lipper & Mann and Napco, all began to copy the style of Holt-Howard's prod-uct line. While each company made creative condiment jars, the Davar Company came pretty close to and practi-cally copied the Pixieware copyrighted design. Although many other companies' jars were different, they were all competing for sales around the same time-frame of the late 1950s and early 1960s. Today, many of these condiment jars have also become highly collectible and some are commanding top dollars at antiques and collectibles shows.

A COLLECTOR IS BORN

My first encounter with Pixiewares was in a hardware store that carried a large line of kitchen-related items. While paying for hardware supplies at the register, I looked up at a row of about 10 Pixiewares adorning a shelf and lined up like soldiers. I decided to purchase four of them as an anniversary gift for my parents. My parents adored the gift. Every day, these pixies were a part of our family meal gatherings in the kitchen. After many years, my folks changed residence to a smaller apart-ment and I was asked to adopt the Pixies.

For years to follow, these four jars were on display in my home and I always had regretted not purchasing more of this now discontinued set (little did I know that there were more than 60 pieces to the set!). It wasn't until friends stopped by one day and mentioned that they saw Pixiewares at various flea markets and collectible shows that I realized that there was a possibility that I could hunt for more of these whimsical novelties. No sooner said than done, the hunt was on and the rest is history.

I guess that I was always a closet collector, but never faced up to it until the Holt-Howard Company came into my life. My very first awareness of the Holt-Howard Company was with my collection of Pixiewares. I never knew what else the company manufactured or sold. As I pursued my hunt for the elusive Pixies, other adorable Holt-Howard novelty ceramics began popping up at collectible shows; a whole new world of collecting opened up for me and thus a collector was born.

THE NEED FOR THIS BOOK

Very little has been written about Holt-Howard and its Pixiewares (in addition to the other companies I mentioned). Many times at collectibles shows and flea markets, I've noticed Pixieware heads on the incorrect jar bottoms and even other companies' jar components mixed with Holt-Howard's product line. After seeing these mix-ups, it became evident to me that a reference guide on this subject was necessary.

Although The Holt-Howard Company was in exis-tence until 1990, the subject matter in this book is basi-cally dedicated to products it created from the late 1950s through the early 1960s. This book is primarily designed to capture the whimsical side of Holt-Howard. I'm pleased to share with you not only Holt-Howard's Pixiewares, but also so many other wonderful Holt-Howard novelty collectibles. Due to the market demand for competing companies' condiment jars, I have also incorporated them into this book in the hope that this information will serve as a tool to educate both collectors and dealers. The historical information within these chapters will enable you to recognize Holt-Howard's product lines and help you differentiate between Pixiewares and other companies' condiment jars.

Just as musical memories from the past touch our hearts, so do these wonderful collectibles of yesteryear. The joy of hunting and finding these nostalgic treasures is truly rewarding. With the turn of the century upon us, these ceramic collectibles of yesteryear are going to hold even more intense memories and historical value for every collector.

ABOUT THE PRICES

The prices in this book were formulated as guidelines and should not to be used to establish an actual fixed price. These prices are a compilation of averages from different parts of the country. Prices vary from region to region. In certain areas of the country, Holt-Howard and other collectibles are more plentiful than in others, so supply-and-demand can affect prices. Scarcity of a highly desirable collectible influences the price that a collector is willing to pay. Rare pieces will always command more money than common ones. Rare pieces are generally the result of limited production of an item or the piece's fragility (causing it to break easily and almost become extinct over the years).

Another factor governing the true value of a piece is condition. Any collectible that is chipped, cracked or faded should not be bought or sold at top dollar, as if it were in perfect condition. As a devout collector, I would rather purchase a rare piece with minor damage than never have the opportunity to possess it again in my lifetime; however, I would not expect to pay top dollar for a flawed collectible.

The cost that a dealer incurs to purchase an item will affect the final resale price. The decision is yours as to whether or not to make the purchase, always bearing in mind that you would like to recover your costs should you decide to part with your cherished possession.

The price guidelines in this book are retail prices— what you can expect to pay for an item from a dealer at a collectibles show or flea market. The prices are not auction prices that appear on the Internet and other sources. Auction prices often involve bidding wars and are not a reflection of true market values.

Also, keep in mind that prices can change. If there is a sudden influx of new collectors with new money, it's possible that the entire Pixieware market could see an increase in values in 1998 and 1999. The values in this book are really a snapshot in time (in this case, the prices are current from when the book went to the printer, which was in early 1998).

As a final note, bear in mind that the publishing world is not a perfect one, and, on occasion, typographical or other unintended errors might sneak into this book. If you see something you believe is in error, please bring it to my attention so it can be corrected in future printings or editions. Neither the author or publisher of this book are responsible for monetary losses that may occur to any person consulting this book for pricing guideline information.

LOOKING FOR YOUR FEEDBACK

Do you have Holt-Howard items or other companies' items that are not listed in this book? If so, I'd like to hear about them for possible inclusion in future editions of this book. You can contact me (Walter Dworkin) through Krause Publications Books Editorial at 700 E. State St., Iola, WI 54990-0001.

Acknowledgments

I want to start by thanking Sara Carbonier of the Colonial Candle Company. Sara was my "key" to the magic kingdom of Holt-Howard and went out of her way to supply me with invaluable information and catalogs. Best of all, thank you, Sara, for introducing me to your dad, Curtis Blanchard, of the former Holt-Howard Company. Curt's tremendous dedication to this book has supplied me with a wealth of historical Holt-Howard information, catalogs and—finally after years of searching—Mr. John Howard himself!

Thank you, John Howard, for taking the time from your busy schedule at Grant-Howard Associates to assist me in this book. All the wonderful interviews, phone calls, catalogs, your incredible support and dedication to this book and especially your friendship. And how wonderful it was of you to introduce me to Grant Holt, whose memories that we shared over the phone were such a tremendous help in completing Holt-Howard's history—thank you, Grant Holt.

Thanks to Darline Comisky, Fred Blair and Esdras Rodriguez, three Holt-Howard collectors who really know the meaning of giving and sharing. Each one of these collectors has shared their collection with me and supplied invaluable photos and background information for this book.

A special thank you to Adam Dworkin, a terrific nephew and a Holt-Howard fan whose computer genius and organizational skills were a tremendous aid in developing this book. Also, my deep appreciation and thanks go out to David and Robin Dworkin for all their help and support.

Fate was shining brightly on me the day I found the photographers for this book. I can't help but express a world of gratitude to Mary and Joe Van Blerck of Van Blerck Photography and Mary Norman of Mary Norman Photography for all their creative talents, photographic expertise and dedication to this book.

Thanks to Diane Bass of Ralph's Collectables, Janet Paruolo and Michelle Carey, I'm eternally grateful not only for all your helpfulness with this price guide, but especially your friendships. Thank you so much for always sharing your collections and your pricing expertise from different areas of the country.

Many thanks to the following individuals who helped with photos or historical information: Joe Feigley, Bill and Florence Bouma, Michael Hall and Pat Glascock, Chris Mahlock, Donna and Steve Wisnewski (Antique Corner), John Clay and Judy Shute (Weather Vane Antiques), Lori Smith, Deanna and Gale Longnecker, Bobbie Zucker Bryson, Evan Pazol, Sharon Spielman, Georgette Stock, Fritz Howe, Ann and Ken Storms, Marlene Krumm Sanders, Connie and Jeff Knecht, Holly Lupfer, Francine Sholty, as well as Barbara Skyer of The Lefton Company.

Very special thanks to all the dealers of collectibles who not only put up with me, but went out of their way to accommodate and help me complete my collections. Thank you one and all: Kathy and Tony Zadjura (Sentimental Journeys), Penny Van Wart and Peter Jones (Penny Toys), Steve and Vera Skorupski (What's Shaking), Gene and Larry Lawrence (G&L Collectibles), Linda Kleinman (Bald Eagle Antique Center), Cookie Katz (Cookie's Collectibles), Ruth Weeks (Borrowed Time), Dawn and Mike Ryder (Dawn's Antiques and Collectables), Fran and Carl Stone (Fran Stone Collectibles), Carol and Dan Walker (Walker's Collectibles), Barbara Strand and Dan Toepfer (Dullsville), Bill Ruman and Tom Kraft (New Options), Michele Bady (MB's Collectables), Maureen and Richard Gorecki (More-Rich-Antiques), Pat and Oliver Williamson, Debbie Gillham, Gerry and Larry's Collectibles, Ellen Bercovici, Edna and Wayne Knight, Bobbie Segal and Kim Becker.

Walter Dworkin was raised in Queens, New York. A graduate of Far Rockaway High School, he attended Queens College in Flushing, New York, as a foreign language major. During his long career with the New York Telephone Company, he served as an assistant engineer and purchasing agent.

In 1994, after 30 years of telephone service, he took advantage of an early retirement incentive and is presently enjoying a second career at a local nursery in Long Island, New York, pursuing his other hobby and second love, horticulture. Walt has served as president and a member of the board of directors of many horticulture societies on Long Island. He has created several new hybrids and is a nationally recognized hybridizer of Begonias. He has written several articles for local and national horticultural organizations; also, *The Brooklyn Botanical Gardens* and *National Begonian* published his experiences on hybridizing Begonias.

Walt has been an avid collector of fine antiques for the past 30 years and is a devout believer of preserving items of yesteryear. Among his antiques interests are furniture, oil paintings, crystal and china. But he also enjoys hunting for and the thrill of finding "fun" items, such as the wonderful ceramic collectibles from the 1950s and 1960s. He claims his sense of humor and love of nostalgia are the key factors that have drawn him into the collecting arena of whimsical holiday and novelty ceramics.

If you are interested in selling or trading Holt-Howard items you can contact Walt through Krause Publications Books Division at 700 E. State St., Iola, WI 54990-0001.

Walter Dworkin

The Howards, brothers John and Robert, grew up in Walpole, Massachusetts. They met Grant Holt of Evanston, Illinois, while all three were students at Amherst College, in Amherst, Massachusetts. Their parents encouraged the three students to go into business for themselves, and their families loaned them $9,000 to do so. John and Robert Howard and Grant Holt started the Holt-Howard Company in 1949 in an apartment on East 35th Street in Manhattan, New York. Not having their own official office, this newly born company used 475 Fifth Ave., in Manhattan as its official mail-drop address. Eventually, as their company grew, these three entrepreneurs remained in Manhattan and located their first official office at 126 E. 28th St., and the company also had a showroom at 225 Fifth Ave., also known as Manhattan's Gift Center Building.

While the three partners all loved to sell, product development and sourcing were the responsibility of Robert Howard; sales management was handled by John Howard; and the financial affairs and office operations were under Grant Holt's supervision. In the early days, the three partners were not basically in the importing business and attempted to conduct all their transactions within the United States. The concentration in the first few years was strictly on Christmas items. John Howard recalled that Holt-Howard's very first successful holiday item was an "Angel-Abra." Shortly after the "Angel-Abra," Holt-Howard's Christmas line became extremely successful and launched this young company on the road to success.

John Howard told me that

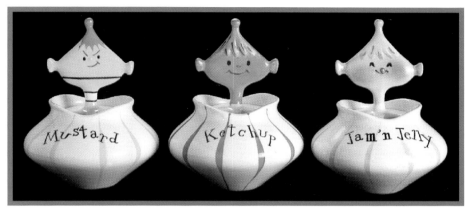

Some of the first Pixiewares (from Dworkin Collection; photo by Van Blerck Photography).

Christmas items were popular (from Dworkin Collection; photo by Van Blerck Photography).

Christmas and kitchen-related giftware items proved to be the most feasible and popular commodities for them in the 1950s. Although Christmas and holiday items were very important to the growth of their company, Holt-Howard did not want to become a seasonal company only, so it branched out into kitchen-related items. The firm's profound belief in the success of kitchen-related items was the catalyst which led to the creation of the famous Pixiewares line. As Holt-Howard continued its expansion into kitchen accessories, it also started

designing Santa coffee mugs and pitchers. According to John Howard, their Santa coffee mugs became so popular that Holt-Howard started creating coffee mugs for daily use. As a result of this success, Holt-Howard was credited with pioneering the invention of the coffee mug as we know it today. Prior to 1950, mugs were not in common usage.

BUSINESS IS BOOMING

With business getting bigger and product lines expanding, manufacturing was becoming very expensive locally. In 1953, Robert Howard traveled abroad and made manufacturing contacts in Japan. Robert Howard informed a fellow co-worker that his travel pioneering efforts abroad were not easy. To begin with, his first trip to Japan in the late 1950s took 48 hours flying in prop planes—DC3s and constellations. The trip included several stops crossing the United States, and then stops in Hawaii, Guam, Wake Island and so on, en route to Tokyo. Even later travel during the mid 1960s was still quite an ordeal: New York to Chicago to Anchorage to Tokyo on a 707. Since Holt-Howard was selling to individual specialty gift shops, top-of-the-line department stores and some mail order, extreme cautions were exercised in selecting only the best manufacturing plants abroad that could meet the company's high quality and production standards. Eventually, Holt-Howard imported decorative and novelty home- and kitchen-related products from more than 20 countries in Asia and Europe.

In 1955, Holt-Howard relocated its headquarters from New York City to Spruce Street in Stamford, Connecticut. Holt-Howard remained a Connecticut-based company, eventually moving to 7 Market St.. and finally 200 Henry St. Even though Holt-Howard had relocated, it still maintained its showroom in New York, and issued new catalogs annually. Holt-Howard was comprised of four companies: Holt-Howard Canada, Holt-Howard West, Holt-Howard International, plus it had 45% ownership of John E. Buck & Co. ltd., in Colchester, England. Its distribution and warehousing centers were located in Stamford, San Rafael (California) and Toronto. During the 1950s, the U.S. West Coast market was much smaller and less feasible for sales development; however, Holt-Howard eventually expanded into California and opened its first showroom in Los Angeles. This later West Coast expansion is perhaps the main reason why Pixiewares and other Holt-Howard collectibles have always been less prevalent on the West Coast than they are on the East Coast.

PIXIEWARES AND BEYOND

In 1958, Holt- Howard was the first company to create and manufacture Pixiewares, a very unique concept in deep glazed condiment containers. These novelty ceramics were designed with whimsical pixie heads that were perched atop each condiment container. Each container's removable head was attached to a lid and spoon and served as the unit's closure. The pixie's head had protruding spoke-like hair and ears that were designed to serve as the handle to each jar's lid.

Pixiewares were copyrighted and soon became an extremely popular collectible. As a result, Holt-Howard began to expand its Pixiewares product line into other related companion giftware items. Pixiewares were not only a huge success in the late 1950s and early 1960s, but are presently enjoying a second life in the 1990s. Whether is collectors' zeal for nostalgia or the fact that Pixiewares are just plain adorable, these whimsical imps are one of the hottest items in today's collectibles marketplace. Dealers of collectibles will tell you that the popularity and public demand for Pixiewares is overwhelming.

Robert Howard's artistic creativity and imagination in designing the facial expressions of his beloved Pixiewares was truly one of the reasons for their huge success. The whimsical pixie faces were very expressive and always represented their container's contents (with a smile, frown, grimace or crying—many even flirted with each other).

Holt-Howard created so many exciting seasonal, all-occasion, and everyday collectibles that it would be impossible to cover all of them in one book. During Holt-Howard's huge success with Pixiewares, the company was also on a whirlwind of producing many other whimsical collectibles. The company's products were not only kitchen-related, and certain product lines were expanded into the bar, den, bath and almost every room in the house.

One of Holt-Howard's most popular product lines was its Cozy Kitten series. How clever to create an entire line of adorable cat collectibles—who doesn't love cats—not to mention collecting them! Holt-Howard created a serviceable Cozy Kitten for almost every room in the house; today, these toms and tabbies are highly sought after. Holt-Howard simultaneously created its Merry Mouse series, which also stole everyone's hearts. The mice, just like the kittens, were a big success (if this was a cat-and-mouse game, then no one played it better than Holt-Howard).

During this time-frame, the famous red rooster (COQ Rouge) dinnerware set was released for thousands of rooster collectors to enjoy throughout the country. Holt-Howard captured so much of nature and wildlife (as well as an adorable, cartoon-like quality) into its novelties that you just couldn't resist purchasing them. From its salt & pepper shakers to its bobbing banks, Holt-Howard knew how to capture an audience.

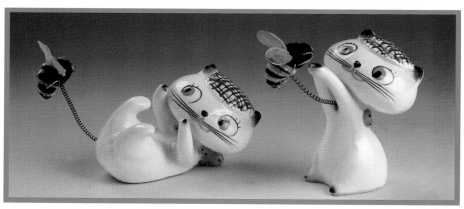

Cozy Kittens (from Dworkin Collection; photo by Van Blerck Photography).

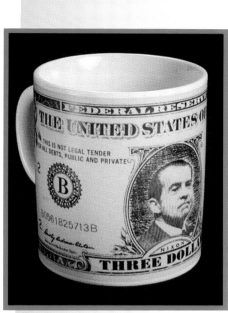

President Nixon coffee mug (from John Howard Collection; photo by Van Blerck Photography).

THE NIXON MUG

While on the subject of capturing an audience, the Holt-Howard Nixon mug certainly captured the entire country's attention in September of 1973! While Holt-Howard was under General Housewares Division, it released a President Nixon coffee mug with Nixon pictured on a $3 bill. This mug created quite an uproar.

This Nixon mug was manufactured in Japan. It pictured former President Nixon on a $3 bill. The sales of this mug were on a whirlwind, until the federal agents of the Secret Service stepped in and informed Holt-Howard that it was in violation of federal currency laws governing "similitude" (resembling in any way the paper money of the United States), and Holt-Howard was notified by the Secret Service to "cease and desist."

Within no time, the Secret Service seized shipments of the mugs at several retail outfits and also

descended on Holt-Howard's warehouses in San Rafael and Stamford, confiscating and smashing 2,000 of the controversial mugs. This mug was also dubbed the "Counterfeit Coffee Cup" and newspapers had headlines that read: "Mugs With Nixon Likeness Busted," "U.S. Seizes Mugs with Picture of Nixon on $3 Bills" and "Tempest Over a Coffee Mug." On Oct. 8, 1973, even *Newsweek* featured a story on this mug entitled, "A Mug's Game." Another newspaper printed that citizens could be prosecuted for possession of a Nixon Mug! Just for the record (should you ever locate a survivor), this mug is copyrighted HH-1972, with an identification number 8321 Japan, and it sold for $1.60 in 1973.

CREATIVITY WAS A HALLMARK

So much for fun and whimsical things, for there was also a very serious and practical side to Holt-Howard as it created, designed and manufactured numerous other kitchen, picnic, household and office-related products.

The creativity in Holt-Howard's advertising was always a joy to see. In the candle holder section of its catalogs, Holt-Howard stated that customers could "grace the glow" of candle light with its beautiful candle holders. The company created all kinds of candle holders, even holders made of wrought iron, as well as ceramic holders equipped with well bases for water to hold fresh flowers. Holt-Howard also invented candle climbers and offered them in a wide variety of figural forms. Candle rings were also displayed to dress up candles and were created in a multitude of flowers, birds, butterflies and other delights of nature.

Beautiful kerosene lamps were illustrated in its catalogs, as well as everything you could possibly want for your flowers and plants, including, planters, wall pockets, various vases and even watering cans.

Dens and desk organizers were always seen in the company's catalogs. There were all types of ceramic organizers for almost every room in

the house and even chrome and ceramic whimsical clips for home or office.

Bar accessories were another Holt-Howard product-line offered in a variety of forms, including decorative fabric liquor bottle toppers (covers), bottles stoppers, condiment jars, decanters and an extensive array of ashtrays and cigarette holders. For the kitchen, there was breakfast and luncheon tableware. Trivets, cutting boards, gourmet cookware, canisters, coffee and tea pots, mugs, creamers, sugars and juice pitchers with matching glasses were just some of the items that were always in abundance and offered to the consumer. For outside the house, Holt-Howard offered many barbecue and picnic accessories, such as aprons, food umbrellas, corn holders and stackable, portable condiment jars.

As you can see, we're looking at a very versatile and energetic company, but it doesn't end here. Most of all, Holt-Howard was always there for us at Christmas, offering a huge selection of holiday decorations and ceramic giftwares. Easter ceramics were also manufactured, but on a smaller scale.

THE END OF AN ERA

Eventually, Holt-Howard was bought by General Housewares Corporation in 1968 and became part of the Giftware Group, along with the Colonial Candle Company. Shortly thereafter, headquarters were moved to Hyannis, Massachusetts, with warehousing facilities in Plymouth. By 1974, the three original partners had left the company. The focus of the new owners changed and the business slowly deteriorated. Finally, in 1990, what remained of Holt-Howard was sold to Kay Dee Designs of Rhode Island. There is no longer a line carrying the Holt-Howard brand name.

John W. Howard remains active managing a housewares importing company called Grant-Howard Associates in Norwalk, Connecticut. Robert J. Howard died in 1990 and A. Grant Holt is retired.

SIGNATURES AND STICKERS

Holt-Howard ink-stamp signed and copyright dated most of its collectibles; however, certain items were not signed and only had a tin foil sticker. In certain tiny collectibles, due to lack of space, it was impossible to sign some of these pieces and occasionally these items may have just read "HH" or nothing at all. Since these collectibles were all made abroad, the word "Japan" would occasionally be part of the ink-stamp signature or at least printed on an accompanying foil label. Occasionally, Holt-Howard would also use numeric identification codes such as 6128L or 6457 to identify its merchandise.

Foil labels were used on many Holt-Howard collectibles displayed in this book, especially collectibles from the late 1950s and early 1960s. The label colors varied from black and gold, silver and gold and red and gold. Most Pixieware pieces all had the black and gold label. The Christmas collectibles usually had the red and gold version of this label; however, during the early 1960s, the rectangular silver and gold was also used.

Black and silver foil label (photo by Van Blerck Photography).

1958 ink-stamp signature (photo by Van Blerck Photography).

Red and gold foil label (photo by Van Blerck Photography).

1958 ink-stamp signature (photo by Van Blerck Photography).

1959 ink-stamp signature (photo by Van Blerck Photography).

Black and gold foil label (photo by Van Blerck Photography).

1960 ink-stamp signature (photo by Van Blerck Photography).

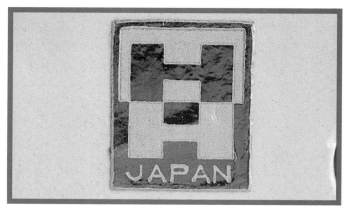

Silver and gold foil label (photo by Van Blerck Photography).

A Word from A. Grant Holt

A. Grant Holt

Talking with people about Holt-Howard, there seem to be two questions that they keep coming back to. First, how did you come to start the business? And secondly, what did Holt-Howard do that was noteworthy? I shall briefly try to answer these questions.

We started in 1949. Bob Howard, John Howard and I had decided while we were in college together that we wanted to own our own business. In the meantime, events had intervened. Bob graduated from college and Harvard Business School and took a job in New York City. John had gone to war, been wounded, recuperated and finished college, while I had finished college, spent a couple of years in the Foreign Service and taken a year of post-graduate work in Sweden.

While studying in Sweden, I found two products which happened to be Christmas items. I contacted the Howards and we agreed we could sell them in the U.S. The first one—a paper Christmas star that hung in the window—we purchased and imported by borrowing $9,000 from our parents, with the proviso that we would pay them back at the end of the Christmas season (and we did). The second product was the Angel Chimes, which we initially called the "Angel-Abra." Since we had no more money to import with, we found a New England manufacturer who would make this product with no money up front. We would pay him after we were paid by our customer. This was a wonderful and

fortunate deal for us, as we didn't have any money to finance this product development.

The Angel Chimes sold very well and is still on the market today. This gave our manufacturer confidence in us and he agreed to make further products for us. While we sold out of the paper star, it was not a strong product and we did not continue it. However, we were launched. Our manufacturer made another successful line of black wrought-iron candleholders for us called the "Andante" line, and a number of metal items, too.

At that time, the state of Vermont had a one-woman government office promoting Vermont craftspeople. Through her, we found a retired Broadway stage designer to decorate large wooden trays for us; a lady who knitted, dressed and stuffed kitten dolls; and a small potter of vases. We were now able to expand our line and make each [sales] call more productive. In 1952, we designed a ceramic product called "Weekend Willie." It was a hollow, unglazed ceramic test-tube-shaped item you stuck into your plant so the water could leak out and give a plant water for an extended period of time. The top was a cute decorated bird's head with its mouth open into which you poured water. We individually gift-boxed it, and Weekend Willie retailed for $1. It was a big winner and gave us extra money to develop our business.

Until 1958, after our initial foray into importing in 1949, we had ceased to import products. However, prices were rising and we were finding it increasingly difficult to make our normal margins with U.S.-manufactured products. Bob Howard's brother-in-law, Bob Pierpoint of CBS fame, suggested we look at Japan as a potential market. We found two Americans who had an export company with offices in Japan and one each in Taiwan and Hong Kong. They introduced us to manufacturers in these markets. Bob was our product-development person and designed nearly everything we sold. As we grew, we hired several other very capable designers to complement Bob. Everything we sold, we designed.

The Far East market was eager for U.S. designs and was willing to do anything we suggested. It was a great opportunity for both sides. We later did the same thing in Italy, Portugal, as well as France and Germany, to a small extent. The key was that we designed and sold new products and new designs. At first, it was in the U.S., and later we expanded into Canada and Great Britain.

What did we do with Holt-Howard that made us different? First, we designed everything we sold. We did not buy "off the shelf" in the maker's showroom. We completely designed our Christmas line and sold it as much as possible to department stores as a complete package. As time went on, we found it increasingly difficult to innovate in Christmas, as there is so much tradition and emotion over home decoration at Christmas. Probably our most important contribution was to show our major retailers that the housewares department could be more than a pots-and-pans and electric department. A kitchen-decor area with a wide variety of useful items (nicely decorated and oftentimes color-coordinated) proved tremendously successful.

We introduced the coffee mug, making it acceptable to use on your breakfast table in place of a cup and saucer. Our wide array of decorated coffee mugs sold strongly to eager consumers who were becoming more casual in their way of life. The housewares store buyer, due to the success of the mugs, was willing to listen to our new ideas. We soon introduced decorated salt and peppers, sugar and creamers, wooden cutting boards decorated on one side, pitchers and soup-and-sandwich sets. In some cases, the same design would cover all products; in others, they were stand-alone designs. It gave us a good variety of product to sell, not only to department stores, but also to gift and specialty shops.

In the 1960s, we were the trendsetters in the housewares area. We ended up having small departments within the housewares department of a number of stores, including Sears, Penney's and Wards. This, in addition to our Christmas line, made our company grow rapidly.

—*A. Grant Holt*

BIOGRAPHY OF JOHN HOWARD

John Howard

John Whitman Howard was born in Cambridge, Massachusetts, on Aug. 3, 1925. He was raised in Walpole, Massachusetts. He entered Amherst College in June of 1943; upon completion of his first semester, he enlisted in the Army. He was assigned to the Army Specialized Training Program. After basic training, the Army's need for infantry became greater than the need for meteorologists, so (with additional training) he was assigned to the First Infantry Division in France. On Thanksgiving Day of 1944, he was wounded by shrapnel in his back and foot in the Huertgen Forest of Germany. Fourteen months of hospitalization followed, after which he returned to complete his education at Amherst.

While at Amherst, his marketing and entrepreneurial interests were nurtured when he and his brother, Bob Howard, formed their first company, Howard Associates (a book sales company), to finance a trip around the country (by selling books). Upon their return, they set up a network of book sales agents in other colleges, including Brown, Dartmouth, Mount Holyoke, Smith and Yale.

In the early days of Holt-Howard, the partners did whatever had to be done, as they were the only employees. As the company grew, John's focus became increasingly on sales and marketing. The objectives were to maximize sales in support of the production runs required by factories to introduce the many new products for which Holt-Howard was becoming known. This led to sales organizations and distribution centers (and eventually separate companies) on the East Coast, West Coast and Canada.

After Holt-Howard was merged into General Housewares. John assisted in putting together the Giftware Group as a separate division of General Housewares. At the completion of a five-year contract, he and Grant Holt decided to become entrepreneurs again and started Grant-Howard Associates, a kitchen gift housewares company. Instead of "HH" on the bottom of products, it became "GHA."

John, whose college objective was to retire at age 45, has found that he enjoys business too much to retire. When Grant Holt retired in 1989, John's son, Douglas, joined the company. Grant-Howard Associates continues to thrive.

John Howard (left) in an interview with author Walter Dworkin in the summer of 1997

Robert Howard

IN MEMORY: BIOGRAPHY OF ROBERT HOWARD

Robert "Bob" Johnson Howard was born in Cambridge, Mass., on May 3, 1923. He showed an early interest in art, which was further developed by art lessons as a youngster and by taking all the art courses he could find in high school and college. At 12, he developed diabetes; while it was a severe case that required twice-daily insulin shots throughout his life, it did not inhibit his work or lifestyle. He received his bachelor's degree at Amherst and a master's in business administration at Harvard.

His first job was in sales at the Strahan Wall Paper Company in 1947, where he was able to use his color and design talents. For a while, he worked two jobs: selling wallpaper during the day and working for Holt-Howard in the evenings in the apartment he shared with his brother, John (which also served as the first offices of Holt-Howard). Bob's genius for sketching designs at the factory level was a unique talent not often seen by factories, particularly in the Far East. Cute and whimsical designs and a great sense for color were his trademarks.

Bob spent two years with Holt-Howard after it merged with General Housewares; he then resigned, feeling frustrated by what he felt was an overly financial focus. He then formed his own product-development company—International Buying Corporation—where he continued to travel around the world, developing products for clients and searching for new factories, particularly in underdeveloped countries.

Bob had a heart attack and passed away in September of 1990 in New York City. His two children, Bob Jr., and Deborah, were working in the business with him. They are now successful entrepreneurs in different businesses, having learned well from their father.

Chapter 2

The 1958 Holt-Howard Pixiewares

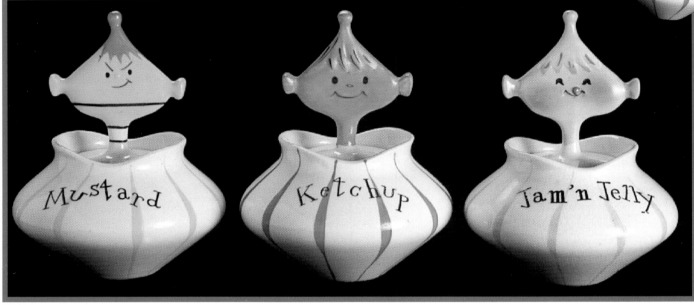

Mustard, Ketchup and Jam 'n Jelly: $45-$55 each (from Dworkin Collection; photo by Van Blerck Photography).

MUSTARD, KETCHUP AND JAM 'N JELLY

In 1958, the Holt-Howard Company introduced what it called "First in the family, Fun characters for table or buffet...yellow striped Mustard, red striped Ketchup, and pink striped Jam 'n Jelly. Head, cover and spoon in one clever unit."

These three whimsical condiment jars were the very first Pixieware pieces created by Holt-Howard. In these pieces is the beginning of the artistic creativity, wonderful styling and detailing of facial expressions that made Pixieware so appealing. The Mustard appears annoyed and unhappy in an effort to conceal his spicy condiment, while his Ketchup and Jam 'n Jelly companions appear to be content. The charm of Holt-Howard's Pixiewares' facial expressions were so adorable that they sparked off an instant love affair with collectors, sellers and gift givers. As the Mustard, Ketchup and Jam 'n Jelly made their debut, their extreme popularity would pave the way to Pixieware stardom throughout America.

Each of these condiments measures 5-1/2 inches high and has 11 colorful vertical stripes around its base (stripe counts varied on individual pieces). Although the Ketchup pixie was advertised as red, the coloration definitely lends itself to a tomato red—more orange in appearance—and should not be confused with the true

red coloration that appears on the later-manufactured Cherries and Chile Sauce jars.

The Mustard, Ketchup and Jam 'n Jelly were sold separately and were individually boxed. They are copyrighted "1958 Holt-Howard." Since these three pieces were the very first pixies created by Holt-Howard, they were the largest production scale of Pixiewares ever, resulting from numerous annual manufacturing cycles of 100-dozen per run from 1958 through 1962. As a result of this mass production, they are the most commonly found pieces today. Forty years have passed since these three pixies made their debut in the 1958 market place. Today, the age and availability of these pieces place them at a market value of $45-$55 each.

Note: Although the Mustard, Ketchup and Jam 'n Jelly were boxed and sold individually by Holt-Howard, they were also featured in B. Altman & Company's 1958 Christmas Catalog and were sold as a three-piece set for $4.95. The huge popularity of these three pixies would soon result in the birth of an entirely new line of Pixiewares and create a new revolutionary concept in condiment jar designs in the late 1950s and early 1960s marketplace.

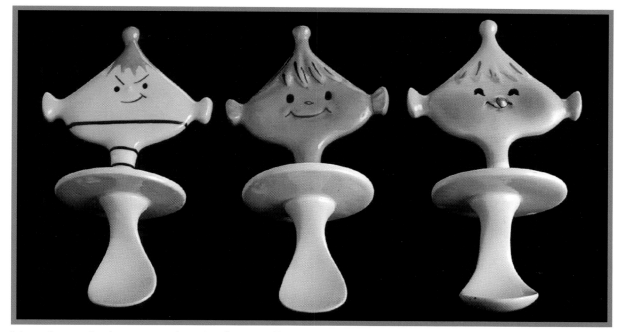

Mustard spoon, ketchup spoon and jam 'n jelly spoon (from Dworkin Collection; photo by Van Blerck Photography).

SPOOFY SPOONS

Holt-Howard gave special attention and employed unique design techniques to its spoofy (meaning hidden) spoons. As you can see, individual considerations were given to each piece to enhance its usefulness. Upon close examination, you can see the clever design of the Mustard and Ketchup spoons, which enables them to serve as spreaders of their condiments. The Jam 'n Jelly's curved spoon is very different—it was designed to scoop and hold its contents. Other pixies were equipped with holes in their spoons to drain liquids, and the Olives pixie even had a spear attachment.

To further capitalize on its successful Pixiewares venture, Holt-Howard introduced numerous brand new additions of pixie giftware items in 1958, creating more kitchen pixies and expanding into bar collectible pixies. These new introductions included the following: condiment jars, soup spoons, stackable seasons, liquor decanters, liquor bottle bracelets and oil-and-vinegar cruets.

INSTANT COFFEE

This adorable impish pixie cousin stands 5-1/2 inches high. She was advertised as "Miss Coffee-Bean Herself." She has a seal-tight, white rubber gasket around her lid which would keep instant coffee air-tight, fresh and dry.

The Instant Coffee pixie wears two light blue bows in her hair—one on top and the other in the back of her head. These bows match the color of her jar's 11 stripes, which was typical of Holt-Howard's color coordination (some element of color in the pixie's head would always match the coloration of condiment jar's base). This color coordination is an insurance to the novice collector that the heads and bases of these pieces are correctly matched.

The Instant Coffee is copyrighted 1958, and today she is hard to find in mint condition. Since her air tight seal functioned so perfectly, it often caused her thin neck to snap at the base as a consequence of consumers pulling on her head to release the seal.

In today's collectible marketplace, this piece is extremely desirable. Because of her coffee-colored face, she is regarded as a crossover collectible by collectors of black memorabilia. This piece is valued from $150-$165.

Instant Coffee (view of bow on back of head and gasket): $150-$165 (from Dworkin Collection; photo by Van Blerck Photography).

Sugar & creamer: $75-$90 for set (from Blair/Rodriguez Collection; photo by Mary Norman).

LIL' SUGAR & CREAM CROCK

Lil' Sugar jar was advertised in Holt-Howard's catalog as follows: "Aqua striped little girl with a little red curl just right for the middle of your table...an any occasion gift."

The phrase Lil' Sugar is very significant here since this pixie is shorter than all of her cousins. She measures 5 inches high—a half-inch shorter than the rest of the Pixieware clan. Although most of her pixie cousins' heads measure 2-1/2 to 2-5/8 inches ear to ear, she has the smallest head, measuring only 2-1/4 inches wide. Accordingly, her sugar bowl is much smaller than the rest of the Pixiewares' bowls. The Lil' Sugar's aqua bow in her hair matches the 10 aqua stripes on her jar. She comes equipped with her very own personalized matching Cream Crock, which measures 2-3/4 inches high; it also has 10 aqua stripes. The Cream Crock was not designed with a pixie head and merely serves as a typical creamer.

This adorable twosome were sold as a three-piece set in box (spoon, sugar bowl and creamer. They are both copyrighted 1958. This piece, along with the Olives jar were two of the first winking pixies to be created by Holt-Howard. The Lil' Sugar's winking eye and smile, accompanied by the serviceability of her Cream Crock, would always make an ideal gift package for anyone's coffee service. This creamer and sugar are valued at $75-$90 per three-piece set.

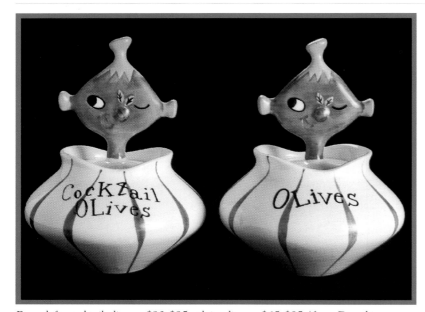

From left: cocktail olives—$90-$95; plain olives—$65-$85 (from Dworkin Collection; photo by Van Blerck Photography).

OLIVES JARS

The Olives pixie was the only Pixieware condiment container designed without a spoon; instead, he was equipped with a stainless steel spear. This piece was displayed in Holt-Howard's catalog with its head levitated above its jar to show off its two-prong steel spear (which may be single-pronged, also).

The Olives was the one Holt-Howard pixie that was responsible for Pixiewares' undeserved nickname of the infamous "Martian heads." Due to the color and shape of his head, unfamiliar flea market dealers labeled him as a Martian, and his pixie cousins would soon be shackled with the same association.

Originally, the Cocktail Olives pixie was part of a bar-set trio that also included Cocktail Cherries and Cocktail Onions. Holt-Howard advertised this set as "party talk provokers." These three pieces were displayed with the first

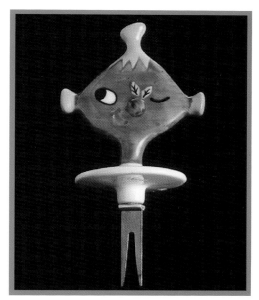

Olive fork (from Dworkin Collection; photo by Van Blerck Photography).

"Happy Party Gremlins" liquor decanters and a four-piece set of pixie liquor bottle bracelets. The Olives, Cherries and Onions condiment containers, accompanied by the pixie liquor decanters and bottle bracelets, comprised a complete and adorable bar-set collectible series.

As time went by, the lettering "Cocktails" was removed from the Olives, Cherries and Onion jars. This change was employed as a marketing strategy to remove the bar and alcohol restriction of these three pieces to allow for more versatility and individual consumer usages.

The Olives pixie, just like the Cherries and Onions heads, wears his own namesake as a nose (an olive with two leaves). His left eye winks, and, if you look closely, his pimento smile is very apparent. This piece stands 5-1/2 inches tall, and his olive-colored head matches the 10 olive stripes on his jar.

The Olives jar was individually boxed. Whether he reads "Cocktail" or just plain "Olives," he is copyrighted 1958. Plain Olives is valued at $65-$85; Cocktail Olives is valued at $90-$95.

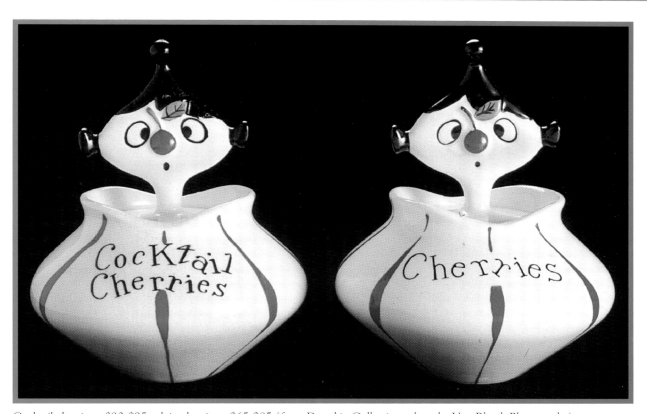

Cocktail cherries—$90-$95; plain cherries—$65-$85 (from Dworkin Collection; photo by Van Blerck Photography).

CHERRIES AND ONION JARS

The Cherries and Onions heads were the only two pixies equipped with a hole in the base of their "Spoofy Spoons." They were designed this way to ensure a drain-dry dripless spoon. This design enabled the spoon to dispense elusive cherries and onions without spilling their juices.

Both of these imps bare their namesakes as noses. The Cherries looks crossed-eyed at his nose, while expressing a look of surprise. The Onion companion appears asphyxiated and on the verge of tears from concealing his overwhelming contents. The Cherries' red nose coloration matches the eight red stripes on its base (this is the only pixie condiment jar with eight stripes). The Onion's green hair, ears

Cocktail onions—$90-$95; plain onions—$65-$85 (from Dworkin Collection; photo by Van Blerck Photography).

Cherries and onions drip-dry spoons (from Dworkin Collection; photo by Van Blerck Photography).

and lined face match the coloration of the 10 green stripes on its jar.

Both of these pieces were originally issued with the lettering "Cocktail" included in their names; however, as mentioned previously, the alcohol association with these pieces was eventually removed. Each piece was individually boxed and copyrighted 1958.

Plain Cherries and Onions are valued at $65-$85 each. Cocktail Cherries and Cocktail Onions are valued at $90-$95 each.

Black-and-white catalog reproduction of the very first original liquor decanters.

300 Proof solid-color base liquor decanter: $175+ (from collection of and photo by Janet Paruolo).

Whiskey solid-color base liquor decanter: $175+ (from Joe Feigley Collection; photo by Richard F. Baker).

LIQUOR DECANTERS: SOLID BASES

Above, we see a black-and-white catalog reproduction of the very first original liquor decanters created by Holt-Howard. These "Happy Party Gremlins" liquor decanters were originally issued with solid-colored deep-glaze ceramic bases. This trio was the only Pixiewares ever issued without striped bases. According to John Howard, the solid-colored liquor decanters, while having a well-coordinated decorative design, were not what the public wanted. Consumers wanted the striped bases that matched and complimented the rest of the Pixieware clan. Within a short time frame, Holt-Howard re-issued these decanters with the famous Pixieware striped bases.

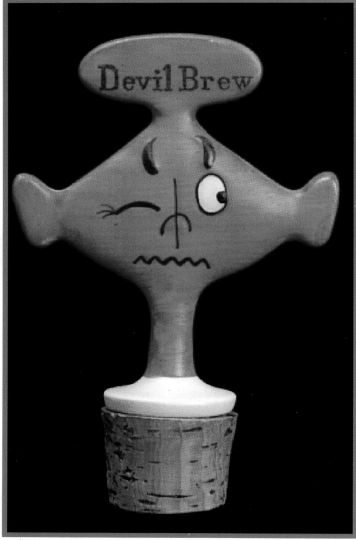

Devil Brew head stopper (from Dworkin Collection; photo by Van Blerck Photography).

these three color photos of decanters could very well be the original "Happy Party Gremlins." Although the "Whisky" decanter's base should be amber colored, it does have an amber glow, and is not as dark as the "Devil Brew's" olive base. John Howard informed me that colors can sometimes vary on these pieces since some of the manufacturing plants in Japan would occasionally exercise minor liberties and slightly alter a product's color scheme.

Although these decanters were always featured in black-and-white photographs, we know that "300 Proof" had a turquoise base to match its pixie head; however, we can only speculate that the "Alcohol" and "Devil Brew" had the same color scheme (amber green or olive green) in solid base, as they later had in a striped base.

Large Pixieware pieces such as these decanters were manufactured in limited production (minimum smaller cycle runs of 300 pieces each, compared to the condiment jars at 100 dozen each). As a result of this limited production, fewer of these liquor decanters were produced and are a rare find in today's marketplace.

To date, the "Alcohol" pixie liquor decanter has never surfaced. Everyone is hoping that one day we will actually see him and know that he exists! Despite their differences, both the "Alcohol" and "Whisky" pixies share a common face; either of them would be the correct stopper head to complete this unique Pixieware bar-set trio.

If the "Alcohol" head was never manufactured,

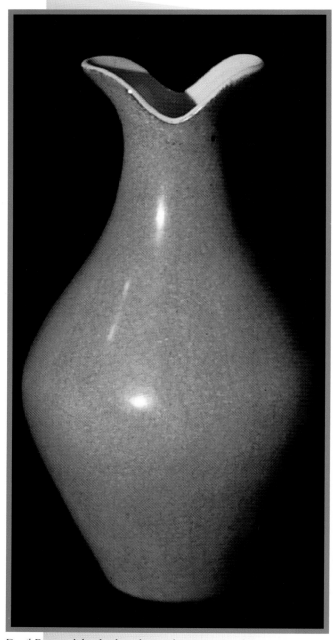

Devil Brew solid-color base liquor decanter, complete with stopper: $175+ (from Blair/Rodriguez Collection; photo by Mary Norman).

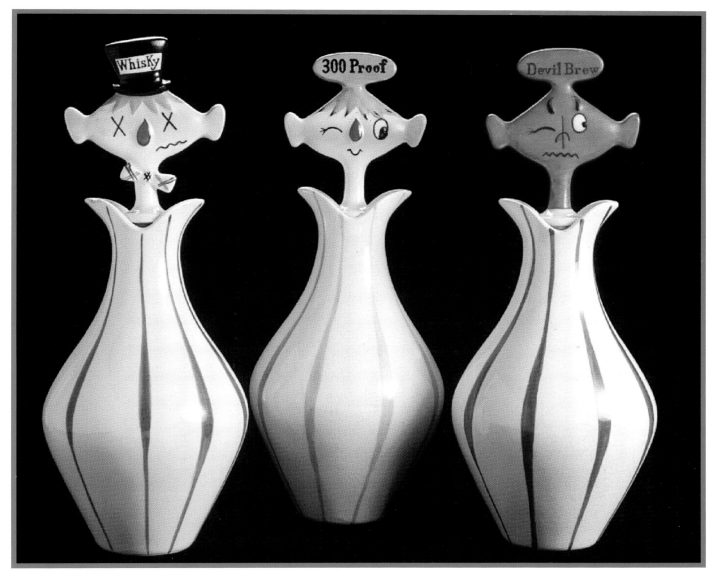

From left—Whisky, 300 Proof and Devil Brew striped liquor decanters: $175+ each (from Dworkin Collection; photo by Van Blerck Photography).

LIQUOR DECANTERS: STRIPED BASES

Once Holt-Howard re-issued this trio with striped bases, it was evident that some minor changes had occurred in the design of the pixies' heads. Upon careful examination of the original black-and-white catalog photo, we notice that the decanter "Alcohol" now became whimsically misspelled "Whisky" and he is wearing a top hat, while his bow tie has become somewhat askew. Decanters "300 Proof" and "Devil Brew" remained the same, except for the arrangement of the lettering sequence atop their heads. This letter arrangement is a minor detail, but worthy of mention to the serious collector.

According to Holt-Howard's catalog, the stripe coloration of the three decanters is as follows: "300 Proof" (aqua striped), "Devil Brew" (olive striped), and "Whisky" (amber striped).

John Howard informed me that the orange paint used on the "Devil Brew's" head was cold paint, and, that

during the manufacturing process, cold paint could not be applied under the glaze; but rather painted over it. This was one reason why the "Devil Brew" pixie probably did not have an orange color-coordinated base. The second reason is that John Howard recalls that his brother Bob, who designed all these pieces, would have wanted a severe contrast between the "Devil Brew's" head and darker base to create a more ominous diabolical design.

Both the solid- and striped-base decanters stand 10-1/2 inches high and are capable of holding about three cups (24 oz.) of brew. Holt-Howard also advertised the decanter bases as performing well as flower vases.

These decanters were not sold as a set and were individually packaged. Both the solid and striped decanters are all copyrighted 1958. All Holt-Howard liquor decanters were manufactured in limited production and are valued at $175+ each.

Four bottle bracelets: $30-$40 each (from Dworkin Collection; photo by Van Blerck Photography).

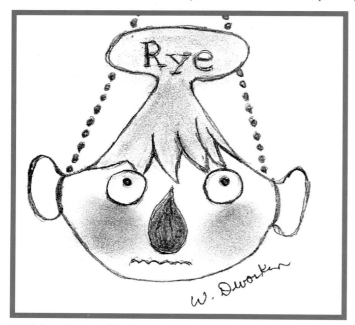

Bottle bracelet, rye: $30-$40 (drawing by Walter Dworkin).

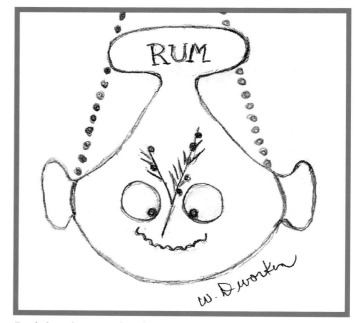

Bottle bracelet, rum: $30-$40 (drawing by Walter Dworkin).

BOTTLE BRACELETS

As part of its cocktail bar line, Holt-Howard also introduced these "Whiskey Whimsey" ceramic liquor bottle bracelets. Each pixie's head was labeled with a specific libation and was designed to mimic the heads in the liquor decanter set. Individual in their own personalities, each little imp's head was attached to a bright brass chain that slipped over one's favorite bottle of liquor.

These bottle bracelets came packaged as a set of four, in a 10-1/2-by-2-1/2 inch rectangular box with a see-through cellophane window. Five different pixie heads were actually pictured in Holt-Howard's catalogs, but it appears that six existed, namely: Rye, Rum, Scotch, Bourbon, Gin and Whiskey. It appears evident that different assortments of four bracelets were on the marketplace when these six pixies were all released in 1958.

Today, these bracelets are hard to find. It can only be assumed, that over the years the majority of these ceramic pieces were ill fated to brake while slipping and sliding over liquor bottles and hitting the glass. These pieces are valued at $30-$40 each.

Sam 'n Sally Salad cruet set (oil & vinegar): $120-$130 each (from Dworkin Collection; photo by Van Blerck Photography).

SAM 'N SALLY SALAD CRUET SET

This adorable pair was named "Sam 'n Sally Salad Set" in Holt-Howard's advertising. They were described as a "a fun way to serve salad fixin's." Both the oil and vinegar jars were equipped with implanted corks and shaker spouts to control the dispensing of their contents, while keeping "Sam' n Sally" neat and clean. In Holt-Howard's original catalog, Sam's head was shown levitated above his jar to show off his spout, and Sally was captioned as saying "don't lose your head, dear." Both pieces have brass fitting rings attached to their necks to hold their heads tight on their bases.

Sally's yellow hair with the lettering "OIL" inscribed on it matches the 10 yellow stripes on her cruet base. Sam's green hair with "VINEGAR" inscribed on it matches his 10 green stripes. Each cruet is 9 inches high and is capable of holding 1-1/2 cups of liquid.

This happy couple stare lovingly at each other and were sold as a pair. They are copyrighted 1958. These pieces are difficult to find in perfect condition and are valued at $120-$130 each.

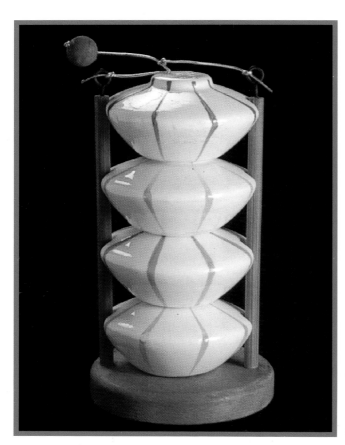

STACKING SEASONS

This set of two salts and two peppers were ingeniously designed (without heads) to be racked for table use and safely portable for picnics or patios. The interlocking structure of the salts and peppers enabled them to be stacked on top of each other. Each shaker has two notches on its sides to lock it into place with the other two supportable wooden dowels. These dowels, when tied together at top, would hold all four stacked shakers securely on their wooden base.

The four colored striped shakers (blue, green, pink and yellow) mimicked and were coordinated to match the Pixieware condiment jars. Each shaker has eight stripes, a cork stopper and seven alphabetically arranged holes punched on top to either identify an "S" for salt or "P" for pepper. The four "Stacking Seasons" were sold as a set, complete with a wooden rack and copyrighted 1958. This set is valued at $55-$65.

Stacking seasons salts & peppers: $55-$65 for set (from Dworkin Collection; photo by Van Blerck Photography).

Disassembled stacking seasons salts & peppers (from Dworkin Collection; photo by Van Blerck Photography).

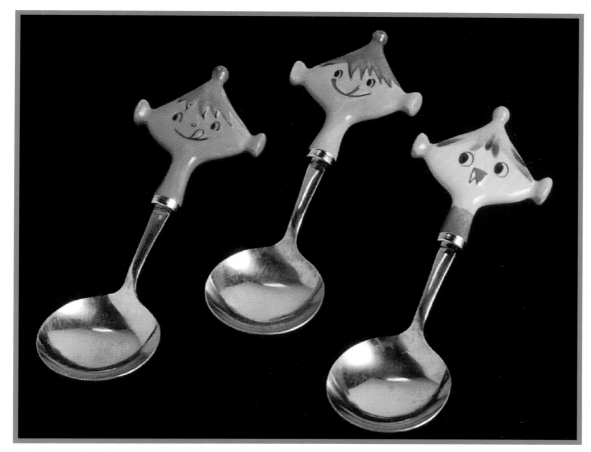

Three spoons: $50-$65 each (from Dworkin Collection; photo by Van Blerck Photography).

SPOONS

Probably four of the cutest ceramic spoons ever created were issued by Holt-Howard in 1958. These pixie flat-headed spoons measure approximately 2-1/4 inches from ear to ear, and 3 inches from their necks to the top of their heads. The entire spoon is 6-1/2 inches long. Holt-Howard advertised this colorful quartet as "whimsical spoons to add color to serving soup 'n stew 'n others too!"

Each spoon is comprised of ceramic-head construction on a stainless steel base. The back metallic portion of the spoons reads "Stainless Steel Japan," accompanied by the famous Holt-Howard paper sticker label on the back side of each pixie's head (these pieces were not signed). These smiling pixie spoons have four different faces, two licking their lips, one sporting a carrot nose and the yellow pixie's mouth almost resembles a beak. One characteristic they share is that all their eyes stare in the same direction. This foursome was colored green, yellow, orange and flesh and was sold as a set of four. The spoons are valued at $50-$65 each.

Spoon: $50-$65 (from collection of and photo by Janet Paruolo).

The 1959 Holt-Howard
Chapter 3 Pixiewares

In Chapter 2, we saw the first of 28 Pixieware pieces that pioneered and greatly impacted the 1958 collectibles marketplace. These eye-catching adorable imps were making their debuts in stores such as B. Altman & Co., specialty giftware shops, top-of-the-line department stores and some mail-orders companies. In an almost overnight success story, the public's demand for Holt-Howard's Pixiewares became very intense and resulted in true super-star status for the pixies. Pixiewares had now become highly collectible and the ideal gift to give and receive.

Pixiewares' rise to fame in one short year stimulated the competitive marketplace and resulted in numerous other companies, both large and small, creating their own line of condiment jars. But unbeknownst to its competitors, Holt-Howard was already introducing a brand new line of more than 30 Pixieware giftware items. Holt-Howard referred to these new introductions as "Cousin's by the dozens" of adorable imps.

Holt-Howard relocated to 639 Canal St., Stamford Conn., and was now preparing its new 1960 catalog for release. This new catalog line of Pixiewares would not only introduce more condiment jars, but would also offer salad dressing jars, shallow bowls, ashtrays, an *hour d'ervous* set, towel hooks, a hanging planter, candle holder hurricane vases and much more

Relish: $95-$110 (from Dworkin Collection; photo by Van Blerck Photography).

RELISH JAR

Upon close examination of the four new 1959 Pixieware condiment jars, you'll notice dimensional style changes in the pixie's heads to more of a diamond shape. The relish jar is the only Pixieware piece of the original 12 jars that has such an elongated head from ear to ear. The peevish expression on his face almost gives you the feeling that he's annoyed because someone pulled on his ears and stretched his face!

If you examine the relish's hairdo, you see the new pixie hairstyle for the 1959 pixies—a rounded, somewhat elliptical balled-end knob. All previous 1958 pixies had spoke-like hairdos (except for the Onions and Olives, which were flat tops).

The relish jar, with his scallion-leafed neck (accompanied by companion pieces, Mustard, Ketchup and Chili Sauce), were sure to have been seen around many barbecue grills during the late 1950s through 1960s. The relish jar's turquoise-colored face matches the stripes on his jar, and he is copyrighted 1959. This piece stands 5-1/2 inches tall and is valued at $95-$110.

MAYONNAISE JAR

It's a very strong possibility that Holt-Howard might have been the only company to ever manufacture this type of a mayonnaise jar. The mayonnaise is a winking pixie, just like some of her other cousins (Honey, Chile Sauce, Lil' Sugar and Olives). An interesting observation in the 1959 pixies is that three out of four are winkers, and their opened eyes always look to their left.

The mayonnaise jar, with her rosy colored cheeks, stands 5-1/2 inches tall. Her butterscotch-colored hair and nose match the stripes on her jar. This piece was individually boxed, copyrighted 1959 and is valued at $95-$110.

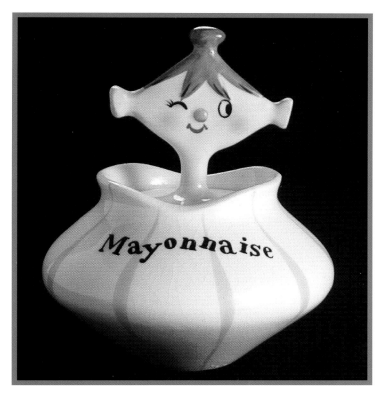

Mayonnaise: $95-$110 (from Dworkin Collection; photo by Van Blerck Photography).

HONEY JAR

This is another winking pixie, but she is the only one of the clan that has a brown eye. This piece and the olives jar are the only pixies whose winking eyes sweep downward in a sleepy closed position, while all the rest of the winking cousins have their winking eyes upright in a flirtatious-type gesture. The surprised expression on the honey's face almost leads one to believe that she is stuck and cannot remove herself from her jar's sticky contents.

Again, Holt-Howard was possibly the only company to manufacture a honey jar of this type. Two rumors concerning the honey jar's scarcity in today's marketplace are certain to be fact: 1) over the years, many honey necks snapped from consumers scooping the heavy sticky honey and the jars were tossed into the garbage; 2) due to Holt-Howard's limited production of this jar, she is a very rare and difficult piece to find.

The Honey jar's yellow face has rosy colored cheeks and stands 5-1/2 inches tall. Her brown hair matches the stripes on her jar. She is copyrighted 1959 and is valued at $300+.

Honey: $300+ (from Dworkin Collection; photo by Van Blerck Photography).

CHILI SAUCE

The Chili Sauce joins the group of her other pixie cousins as being one of the five original winking condiment jar pixies. This piece is the only one out of the original 12 condiment jars that has a differently designed base. This jar was not only designed with 10 vertical stripes, but was also lined with sets of six black oval droplets between its stripes. These droplets are supposed to be indicative of spilled-over dried Chili Sauce.

The Chili Sauce's heart shaped lips match her jar's stripes, while her blushing red cheeks and ears have the appearance of being air brushed and are more of a lighter red. Once again, due to limited production in 1959, the Chili Sauce is probably the second most difficult piece to find today (compared to the honey jar). This piece stands 5-1/2 inches tall, is copyrighted 1959 and carries a value of $175-$185.

Chili sauce: $175-$185 (from Dworkin Collection; photo by Van Blerck Photography).

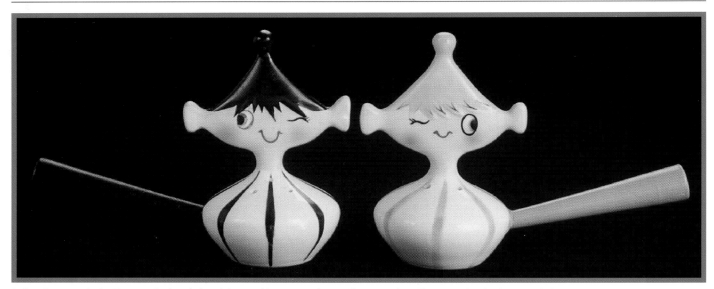

Salty & Peppy (salt & pepper): $175-$185 for set (from Dworkin Collection; photo by Van Blerck Photography).

SALT & PEPPER SHAKERS

This cheerful winking pixie duo salt-and-pepper set was named "Salty & Peppy" in Holt-Howard's 1959 catalog. Both pieces are equipped with unique wooden handles which are painted and color coordinated to match the eight colorful vertical stripes on each pixie's shaker. The purpose of these handles, of course, was to turn "Salty & Peppy" upside down to shake and pour out their contents. The handles are glued into each pixie's shaker.

Each shaker is equipped with a rubber stopper on the bottom to plug and hold in its contents. Salty has three frontal holes, while Peppy has two holes. This adorable couple are signed under their bases, with the © and only the letters "H.H." (the name Holt-Howard is not spelled out). The H.H. paper sticker covers their stoppers. The pair are not dated, but were part of the 1959 year Pixieware releases. They stand 4-1/2 inches tall and are a rare find. "Salty & Peppy" are valued at $175-$185 per set.

Party Pixies hors d' oeuvre dishes: $150-$165 each (from Dworkin Collection; photo by Van Blerck Photography).

Party Pixies Hors d' oeuvre Dishes

This adorable *hors d' oeuvre* set couple were referred to as "Party Pixies" and also "Pretzel Pixies," in two of Holt-Howard's catalogs. The girl pixie was illustrated showing off *hors d' oeuvres* in her underplate, toothpicks in her body, and her elongated hairdo stacked and filled with pretzels (hence the name "Pretzel Pixies"). These pixies' extra large ears help support the stacking of goodies on their heads.

Both the boy and girl pixies have six traditional Holt-Howard vertical stripes on their bodies, accompanied by 18 perforated holes (three between each stripe) to insert and hold toothpicks. For easy cleaning, each pixie is removable from its 5-3/4 inch diameter under-plate by a metallic brass screw and nut. Each underplate base has 12 vertical stripes.

This flirtatious couple stare lovingly at each other; although the girl pixie has rosy cheeks, the boy is actually blushing both on his cheeks and ears! It's obvious that this duo were created to be together and accordingly were sold as a pair.

Each of these pieces stands 7-1/2 inches tall. The girl's pink bow on top of her 4-inch hairdo matches the colored stripes on her body and underplate. The boy's green 4-inch hair matches the colored stripes in his body and underplate. This dynamic duo are copyrighted 1959 and are valued at $150-$165 each.

Snack Pixies Set

In a very successful endeavor to market more versatile Pixieware pieces, Holt-Howard created Pixieware shallow bowls in 1959. There were 10 bowls in the set: seven are snack pixies and three are sundae servers. Holt-Howard gave each one of its snack pixies its own characteristic name that was indicative of the piece's functionality: Mustard Max, Ketchup Katie, Pickle Pete, Onion Annie, Olive Oscar, Tartar Tom and Peanut Butter Pat.

These whimsical names were a very clever advertising strategy and almost seemed to animate each piece with its own personality and usefulness. These bowls featured handle heads and were a fun way of serving condiments on your hamburgers, frankfurters and fish, or just to add some smiling faces to your lunch or dinner table. As always, the coloration in each snack pixie's hair or some facial characteristic would always match the vertical colored stripes on its bowls. Occasionally, a bowl's stripe color would match its purpose, i.e., red stripes for ketchup, yellow for mustard, green for olives, and so on.

All pieces are copyrighted 1959 and were boxed and sold individually. These snack pixies are valued at $95-$110 each.

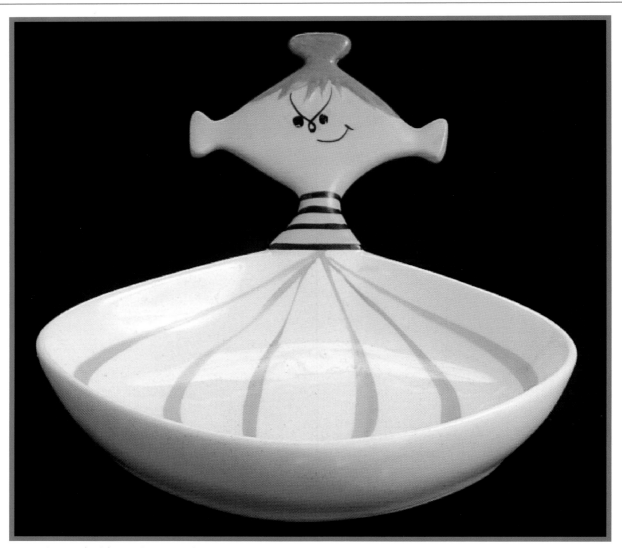

Mustard Max: $95-$110 (from Dworkin Collection; photo by Van Blerck Photography).

Mustard Max

In Mustard Max, we definitely see a color design similar to the 1958 mustard condiment jar. Mustard Max has the orange hair and similar black stripes on his neck as his mustard predecessor; however, he is more of a butterscotch color. Upon close scrutiny, we can see the same cute peevish facial expression that is so prevalent on the relish jar's face.

Ketchup Katie: $95-$110 (from Dworkin Collection; photo by Van Blerck Photography).

KETCHUP KATIE

Ketchup Katie has the true tomato red coloration of the 1958 Ketchup condiment jar. She has three ornamental black buttons that adorn her neck. Ketchup Katie and Mustard Max were pictured together in Holt-Howard's catalog; even though it appears that these two companions belonged together, they were not sold as a pair.

ONION ANNIE

Onion Annie has a true onion-striped face, just like her 1958 predecessor onion jar. Her crossed and slanted eyes and red nose indicate that she is asphyxiated from her overwhelming task of serving onions. Annie's neck is decorated with two green onion leaves that serve as her collar.

Onion Annie: $95-$110 (from collection of and photo by Janet Paruolo).

PICKLE PETE

Pickle Pete bears his namesake as a nose, and, in true Pixieware fashion, he stares cross-eyed. His hair coloration matches the coloration of his bowl's stripes.

Pickle Pete: $95-$110 (from Dworkin Collection; photo by Van Blerck Photography).

OSCAR OLIVES

Oscar Olives is one of the most vividly colored snack pixies with his olive-green face and turquoise stripes. As he stares cross-eyed at his pimento nose, you can't help but notice a family facial resemblance to the 1958 cherries jar.

Oscar Olives: $95-$110 (from Dworkin Collection; photo by Van Blerck Photography).

PEANUT BUTTER PAT

Peanut Butter Pat truly advertises her functionality in living color of peanut butter tan. She carries out one of the family Pixieware traditions as being a winking pixie. Her rust-colored hair contrasts beautifully with her tan stripes.

Peanut Butter Pat: $95-$110 (from Dworkin Collection; photo by Van Blerck Photography).

TARTAR TOM

Although Tartar Tom bears a strong resemblance to his cousin "Pickle Pete," his main functionality was to serve tartar sauce. His turquoise hair and stripes contrast beautifully with his blushing cheeks and beige face.

Tartar Tom: $95-$110 (from collection of Joe Feigley; photo by Richard F. Baker).

This trio was also released in 1959, as part of the original 10 serving bowls. These little imps were specifically designed to accommodate and provide "fixin's" for ice cream sundaes. The design element that differentiates them from their snack pixie cousins is the bow tie around their necks. Each bow tie spells out the functionality of each piece, such as "Nuts," "Berries" or "Goo."

The sundae servers are 5 inches wide and can also be used to serve other desserts such as puddings or pies. Each of these three pieces was sold individually and copyrighted 1959.

Nuts: $95-$110 (from Dworkin Collection; photo by Van Blerck Photography).

NUTS

This sundae server's whimsical olive green face matches the coloration of his bowl's six stripes. His bow tie is decorated with seven olive-green polka dots and black letters which spells out "Nuts." This pixie's deliberately crossed eyes comically demonstrates that he is actually faking being "nuts" and just wants to bring a smile to your dinner guests.

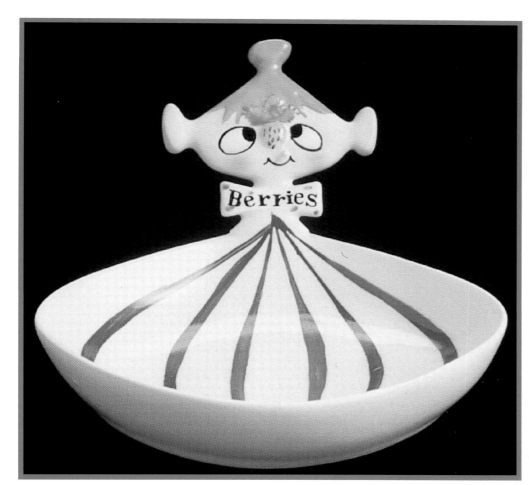

BERRIES

This berries server is a very vibrant and colorful pixie. Here again, in true Pixieware tradition, he stares cross-eyed at his pink and red strawberry-type nose. He has blushing cheeks and a pink tongue that licks his lips in delight. His bow tie states his purpose, and he has six green polka dots that match the coloration of the leaves on his nose. The red dots on his berry nose match the color of his bowl's stripes.

Berries: $95-$110 (from Dworkin Collection; photo by Van Blerck Photography).

Goo: never been located (this photo is from a Holt-Howard catalog).

GOO

After a nationwide search, "Goo" is one pixie that has never been located, and this black-and-white reproduction is all that's available. He's the only one of this sundae trio that is not cross-eyed. This pixie's bow tie appears to have numerous polka dots and spells out "Goo" (defining any delicious ice cream toppings). He also licks his lips.

Tea pot candle-holder hurricane vase, boy: $165-$180 (from Dworkin Collection; photo by Van Blerck Photography).

TEA POT CANDLE HOLDER HURRICANE VASES

This pair of pixie tea pots was designed not only to perform the function of candle holders, but also to serve as vases for cut flowers. Each piece is equipped with an insert for holding a candle and is encased with a clear glass hurricane lamp to surround the burning candle. The tea pot portion can hold water and has six tear-drop shaped holes in the center of each pot to accommodate cut flowers.

Each tea pot has eight traditional Pixieware stripes—one has aqua stripes and the other has pink.

Each piece has a full-bodied color-coordinated pixie resting on its handle that gazes upward at the glass hurricane lamp. The pixies pose in two different positions: the boy aqua pixie's front leg is slightly raised, while the pink girl pixie's rear leg is raised very high. The girl pixie wears a green bow in her hair.

The candle holders stand 8-1/4 inches tall (including the hurricane globe), were sold individually and are copyrighted 1959. These pieces are valued at $165-$180 each (complete with globe).

Tea pot candle-holder hurricane vase, girl: $165-$180 (from Dworkin Collection; photo by Van Blerck Photography).

Salad dressing (Russian, French, Italian), flat heads: $105-$115 each (from Dworkin Collection; photo by Van Blerck Photography).

SALAD DRESSING JARS (FLAT HEADS)

This smiling trio of salad dressing jars are the flat-headed pixies (there was also a set of round heads) salad dressing jars. Each one of these distinguished fellows has a face and hat that is somewhat indicative of his country of origin: Russia, France and Italy. A snug fitting cork is located at the base of each head to plug into the jar and keep the dressing fresh and spill-proof. Each dressing jar comes equipped with its own built-in spout to pour out its contents.

All three containers have eight vertical stripes and hold about 8 ounces (one cup) of liquid. The Italian's green hat matches his jar's stripes, the Russian's neck (stopper) matches his stripes, and the French man's nose matches his red stripes. All three pieces have very differently decorated necks (stoppers). The Italian stopper is orange with black polka dots—the orange color matches his orange nose and mouth; the Frenchman wears a black tie with two black buttons on a light gray stopper; and the Russian stopper is unadorned and butterscotch in color.

Each piece in this dynamic trio stands 7 inches tall and is copyrighted 1959. These three dressings were sold as a six-piece (tops and bottoms) set. When properly displayed as a three-piece set, the Russian looks left, the Italian looks right, and they both stare at their winking French companion in the center. These flat-headed salad dressing pieces are valued at $105-$115 each.

Salad dressing (Russian, French, Italian), round heads: $95-$100 each (from Dworkin Collection; photo by Van Blerck Photography).

Salad Dressing Jars (Round Heads)

This generically altered trio of the original dressing jars are the only three round-headed Pixieware pieces ever manufactured by Holt-Howard. These three round heads are truly atypical of the rest of the Pixieware flat-headed clan; however, upon careful examination we can definitely see a family resemblance to the rest of their cousins.

Although there is a parallel in appearance among these three gents and their predecessors, we can't help but notice drastic changes in the Russian and French pieces. The Frenchman now has blond hair and a mustache, he's lost his white chef's hat and bow tie, and now has an orange-striped jar instead of red. Our Russian fellow is now wearing a black hat and sporting a huge rust-colored beard and mustache, while his jar's stripes are now tan colored instead of butterscotch yellow.

Truly atypical of Pixieware fashion and design, the Russian and French round heads do not exhibit any colors on their heads that match up with their jars. Perhaps the least effected piece from this structural redesign is the Italian dressing. Although there are minor changes in his hat design and color and he now wears a black bow tie, the Italian dressing still bears a resemblance to his flat-headed predecessor. His hat and vertical stripes are now a true green color instead of olive green, and, in true Pixieware fashion, the color of his hat matches the stripes on his jar. There are also many other structural changes in the round-headed design of this salad dressing trio:

- The round head's jars are 1/4 inch shorter than the flat heads.
- Round-headed jars have only seven vertical stripes compared to that of eight on the flat heads.
- The ears of the round heads are smaller and more rounded than the larger pointed ears of the flat heads.
- All three round heads have flesh colored noses instead of the whimsical red and orange noses of their flat-headed cousins.
- All three round heads have eyes that stare in the same direction (to the left), whereas their predecessors did not.
- Round heads have circular lips expressing concerned emotions, rather than the large smiling lips of the flat heads.

Even though the round-headed trio exhibits many structural and design changes, they are also copyrighted 1959, the same as the flat-headed versions. These pieces are valued at $95-$100 each.

Two table favor Pixies, serviettes: $55-$65 each (from Blair/Rodriguez Collection; photo by Mary Norman).

Table favor Pixie, serviette: $55-$65 (from Dworkin Collection; photo by Van Blerck Photography).

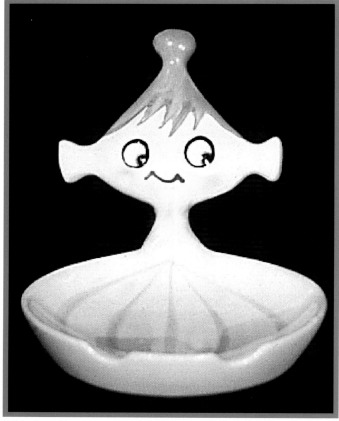

Table favor Pixie, serviette: $55-$65 (from Blair/Rodriguez Collection; photo by Mary Norman).

TABLE FAVOR PIXIES (SERVIETTES)

These table favor pixies were sold as a set of four and were referred to as "Serviettes." Many collectors today refer to them as ash trays, spoon rests, tea bag holders and nut bowls. In reality these adorable imps can serve all of these functions. Each 3-inch wide Serviette is very versatile for table service, and all have two cut-out areas at their front ends to accommodate cigarettes.

The pixie's head can be used as a handle to pass its bowl's contents about the table or for quick cleaning up of cigarette ashes or used tea bags. These Serviettes have a similar hairdos, but each one has a different hair color, and all have different color stripes. These rosy-cheeked pixies are copyrighted 1959 and are valued at $55-$65 each.

Hanging Pixie planter: $175+ (from Dworkin Collection; photo by Van Blerck Photography).

HANGING PIXIE PLANTER

It's rare that you ever see a full bodied Holt-Howard pixie in the flesh (except on the tea pot candle holders), but here we see one climbing the chains of Holt-Howard's only Pixieware planter. This ceramic pixie measures 2-3/4 inches long from head to toe. She sports a flesh-colored body and rosy cheeks and has burnt-orange hair and ears. This hard-working imp's main function is two fold: 1) to wrap her arms around the three 9-inch-long brass chains to gather them together; and 2) to act as an adjuster, sliding up and down the chains to lock the opening into place to accommodate the size of the container's plant.

The ceramic planter bowl has 10 pink vertical stripes, and sweeps up into two points above its rim. The rim is equipped with three holes to hold the chains. Although this planter mimics the bases of the condiment jars, it is actually wider and measures 13 inches in circumference (at center) and 2-1/2 inches in diameter at its opening rim. This item was sold as a three-piece set, including bracket. The entire piece measures 12 inches long (including the chains) and is copyrighted 1959. This planter is valued at $175+.

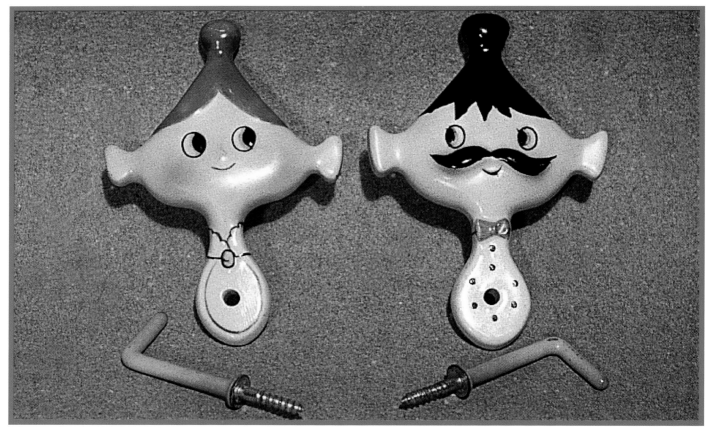

Towel hooks, mother and dad: $50-$55 each (from collection of and photo by Hall/Glascock).

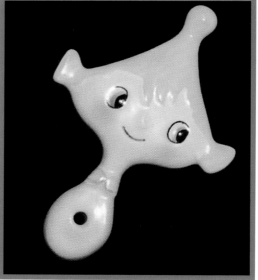

Towel hook, brother (far left) $50-$55 (from Dworkin Collection; photo by Van Blerck Photography).

Towel hook, sister (left), $50-$55 (from collection of and photo by Darline Comisky).

TOWEL HOOKS

While trying to keep up with something new in kitchenware-related items, Holt-Howard created these four smiling pixie hooks. Each pair of pixies smiles lovingly at each other and were equipped with hooks which made them great for hanging dish towels, pot holders or other items.

Both the Mother & Dad and Brother & Sis towel hooks are flat and are 4 inches high. Each piece has a rectangular opening behind the figure's head (for a nail) to hang the piece onto a wall. The base of each figure has a drilled-through hole that accommodates a screw hook to secure the piece and prevent it from sliding.

The Mother & Dad Hooks and Brother & Sis Hooks were sold as separate sets and each were gift boxed. All four pieces are copyrighted 1959. These pieces are valued at $50-$55 each.

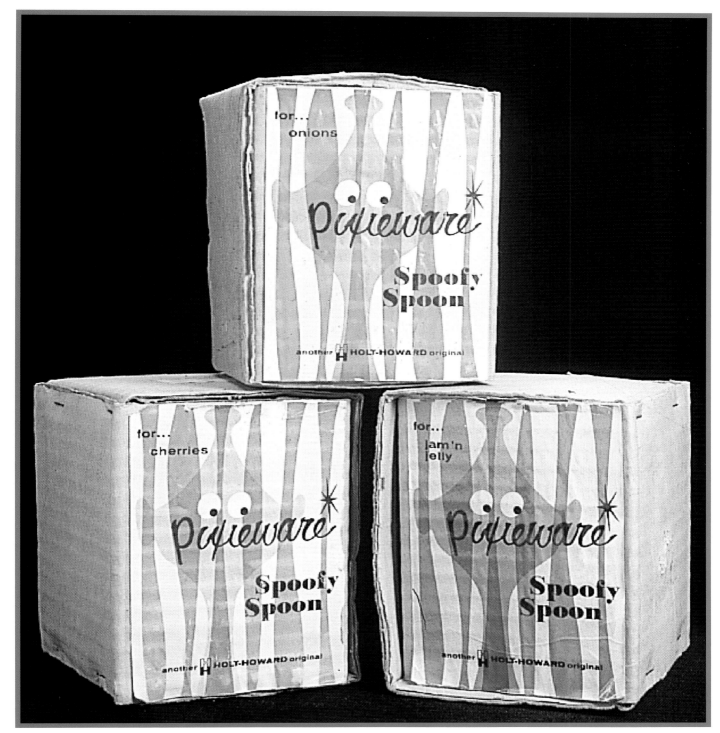

Original boxes that held the condiment jars (from Dworkin Collection; photo by Van Blerck Photography).

ORIGINAL BOXES

The majority of the original 12 condiment jars were sold in the above boxes, this packaging featured a pink Martian-like head and vertical orange stripes which symbolized the famous Pixieware stripes. Each box was individualized only in the upper left corner where the specific condiment jar's name was posted. There was also a corresponding four-digit catalog identification number on a white label (1-1/4 by 2-1/4 inches) which read, "Made in Japan." There was always a big plug for the "Spoofy Spoon" on each box. The inside of each box was cushioned with wood shavings that resembled straw, while each pixie head and its jar were wrapped separately in tan colored tissue paper.

John E. Beck & Co. ltd., catalog page.

John E. Beck & Co. ltd., catalog page.

John E. Beck & Co. ltd., catalog page.

John E. Beck & Co. ltd., catalog page.

THE BRITISH PIXIEWARES

During one of my interviews with John Howard in the summer of 1995, I was going through some old Holt-Howard catalogs, and I was shocked to discover another crop of Pixiewares. These were British Pixiewares and were all featured in a Christmas catalog of John E. Beck & Co. ltd., of Wellington, London, England. Mr. Howard informed me that Holt-Howard owned a 45% interest in John E. Beck and that some of the Pixiewares were re-designed for the British marketplace, especially the creation of a marmalade jar and the addition of a new salt and pepper set.

Although we see many familiar faces in the British Pixiewares, most of their names have been changed or modified. According to Mr. Howard, John E. Beck & Co. ltd., did not have a license to import from Japan in the late 1950s and 1960s; consequently, these British Pixiewares were manufactured in England and Portugal.

Upon careful examination of the Beck catalog page, we can notice the changes between U.S. Pixieware vs. British Pixieware. The U.S. Russian, French and Italian dressing jars became England's oil, vinegar and dressing jars. The U.S. mustard became marmalade, and the jam 'n jelly became jelly and also honey. There was only one Pixieware shallow bowl manufactured in England. We recognize this bowl as Peanut Butter Pat, and she was advertised as a nut bowl.

46

The Davar Company had its principal location in New York County and was located in Manhattan at 15 W. 26th St., New York, NY 10010. This novelty-products company filed its Certificate of Incorporation on Feb. 18, 1957, and began to manufacture and import from Japan a wide range of condiment jars, liquor decanters and associated giftware items. The company was dissolved as of March 24, 1992.

Davar was probably the only other company that used pixies as its main character theme in the design of its knock-off condiment jars. Almost all other companies created fruit-vegetable- or human-type heads as the closures to their jars. Davar copied the Holt-Howard Pixieware line so closely that, even today, collectors are confused between the original Pixiewares and these knock-offs.

In the next couple of chapters, it is my intent to clearly and simply identify and demonstrate the differences between the original Pixiewares created by Holt-Howard and all the other various knock-offs created by numerous competing companies thought the United States. The Holt-Howard Company was the creator and copyrighted owner of the name "Pixieware." Accordingly, we must bear in mind that even though Davar manufactured pixies, also, we should not confuse the nomenclature "Pixieware" when referring to the Davar product line.

DAVAR PIXIES HAD FLAT HEADS

All Davar Pixies are flat heads and somewhat thicker than Holt-Howard's. Although the Davar pixies were adorable in their own right, there was no presence of diversified creativity among the pieces. All pieces were created with flesh-colored faces with minor modifications in their hair styles. The individual pixie's hair color was sometimes color coordinated to match the stripes on its base, but this was not always the case.

The four stripes on each Davar pixie's jar were always horizontal, compared to Holt-Howard's Pixiewares whose stripes were always vertical. One very interesting design feature in the Davar jar was the company's use of flesh-colored pixie arms (often found on sugar bowls) which could be used as handles. Inexplicably, the Davar pixies were made with two different styles of condiment lettering: one in script and the other in print. All the jars with print have erect hairstyles that form a point, while the script jars have short ponytails that flop off to one side.

EACH HAD SPOON

All Davar pixie heads were equipped with spoons. These spoons were styled identically, with no difference in

shape or added features like drainage holes. The necks of the pixies were decorated with two black necklace-type lines. The size of these pixie's heads were not always standardized or compatible with other bases of the same product line. For example, sometimes one ketchup head would be somewhat larger than another and would not fit properly onto another jar of the same type condiment.

More often than not, Davar signed and copyrighted its products; however, today, many of this company's pieces are turning up without signatures or identifying foil labels. The script pixies are generally signed: however, the print pixies are not. From what we have seen in circulation today, it appears that this line of condiment jars was limited and no where as large in scope as the Holt-Howard Pixiewares.

All Davar pixies are copyrighted 1959 only. Many also had a red- and gold-lettered foil label affixed to their bottoms that read, "Davar Originals Japan." The signature "O" with a "V" inscribed over it is another Davar trademark and was found on the oil & vinegar jars; it mimics the shape the foil label and the large letter "V" in "DaVar."

IDENTIFYING DAVAR PIXIES

When shopping at local flea markets and collectibles shows, the novice collector can always identify Davar's pixies by the following characteristics:

1. All Davar pixies have flesh-colored faces only.

2. The stripes on the condiment's container are always horizontal (the condiments have four stripes and the oil and vinegar have nine).

3. Each container has two flesh-colored arm handles (except the oils and vinegars).

4. All Davar pixies are flat heads.

5. All the pixie faces have round red noses.

Mustard (print and script): $45-$50 each (from Dworkin Collection; photo by Van Blerck Photography).

MUSTARD (PRINT AND SCRIPT)

These are two quite unhappy Davar mustard Pixies, each demonstrating their stereotypical Davar flesh-colored faces. The mustards have black stars for eyes, and their yellow hair matches the stripe coloration of their bases. Notice the mustard with the "print" name has an erect pointed hairdo, while its script twin has a plopped-over ponytail. This hair-style treatment is commonplace in all of Davar's pixies. In comparing this pair with the Holt-Howard mustard, we can see the same type of annoyed facial expression. Value: $45-$50 each.

Ketchup (print and script): $45-$50 each (from Dworkin Collection; photo by Van Blerck Photography).

KETCHUP (PRINT AND SCRIPT)

This cheerful twosome has red-colored pixie hairdos to identify each as the correct heads for the ketchup bases. Although their red hair does not match their jar's green stripes, their hair color does match the red lettering "Ketchup" identifying their jars' contents. The flesh-colored arms on these condiment's serve as handles and are standard design on all Davar Pixies. The Ketchup jar is inscribed in red lettering instead of black. Value: $45-$50 each.

Jam 'n jelly (print and script): $45-$50 each (from Dworkin Collection; photo by Van Blerck Photography).

JAM 'N JELLY (PRINT AND SCRIPT)

These Jam 'n Jelly Pixies have big smiles, sleepy eyes and green pixie hairdos. One interesting characteristic about them is that their green hair doesn't match anything on their bases, so the novice collector could never be sure if these heads were matched up correctly. Many times, this pair's hair coloration can vary from light to very dark green; however, they are the correct match for the Jam 'n Jelly base. The four purple stripes around their bases could be indicative of symbolizing grape jelly. Value: $45-$50 each.

Cocktail cherries (print and script): $65-$75 each (from Dworkin Collection; photo by Van Blerck Photography).

COCKTAIL CHERRIES (PRINT AND SCRIPT)

These pixies have triangular-shaped eyes that stare upwards as if perplexed. Their black hairdos are not color coordinated with their gray-striped bases. All the Davar pixies (except ketchup) have their condiments inscribed in black letters (similar to Holt-Howard); however, the bar-set trio also has additional condiments inscribed in red for "cherries," yellow for "onions" and green for "olives." Value: $65-$75 each.

Cocktail onions (print and script): $65-$75 each (from Dworkin Collection; photo by Van Blerck Photography).

COCKTAIL ONIONS (PRINT AND SCRIPT)

One nice feature that this duo has in common is that its blue hair matches the four stripes on its jars, so the inexperienced collector can realize that there is a match. The word "onions" is painted in yellow. Value: $65-$75 each.

Cocktail olives (print and script): $65-$75 each (from Dworkin Collection; photo by Van Blerck Photography).

COCKTAIL OLIVES (PRINT AND SCRIPT)

Here again, we see a color coordination match between the pixie's hair coloration and the four tan stripes around its base. Value: $65-$75 each.

Oil & vinegar (script): $100-$115 each (from Dworkin Collection; photo by Van Blerck Photography).

OIL & VINEGAR (SCRIPT)

This duo proves and exhibits that there is a difference between the hairdos on the printed and script jar heads. Here, we see the proof that script jars heads have hairdos with plopped-over pony tails. We know that these are the correct heads because their striped collars are removable and match the color of their bases. The vinegar's blue hair and collar stripes match his base, while the oil's red collar stripes match her base. The vinegar has stars for eyes and a frowning mouth, while the oil has closed eyes and a very contented smile. Value: $100-$115 each.

Oil & vinegar (print): $100-$115 each (from Dworkin Collection; photo by Van Blerck Photography).

OIL & VINEGAR (PRINT)

Here is the print lettering version of the same couple—notice the difference in their hairdos (erect).

This red-haired vinegar has actual eyes instead of stars as its script counterpart; accordingly, the oil has triangular eyes instead of the closed eyes on its blonde script counterpart. These pieces stand 8 inches high and come equipped with corks inside their collars to hold their heads on tight and to seal their contents. Their bases have nine stripes, and their collars have two thin and two bold stripes that match. Each jar can hold 9 ounces (more than one cup) of liquid.

The oil & vinegar sets in this series were issued by Davar in at least three different color schemes. There is also another color scheme of an all black vinegar and yellow striped oil. Value: $100-$115 each.

OTHER COLLECTIBLE DAVAR ITEMS

As far as we know, these above-mentioned pieces were the only pixies created by Davar; however, there are other Davar pieces that are very collectible in today's marketplace and are worthy of mention in this chapter.

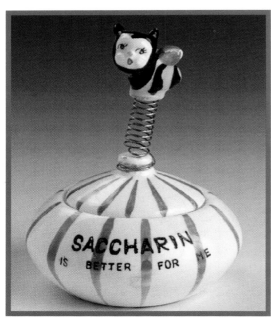

Saccharin: $75-$85 (from Dworkin Collection; photo by Van Blerck Photography).

SACCHARIN

Davar created this small jar entitled "Saccharin Is Better For Me." A little bee is perched atop a small spring and dances with delight every time its jar is touched. The entire piece stands 3-3/4 inches high (including bee) and is 3 inches in diameter at its widest point. The container's mouth opening is 1-1/2 inches across. This piece has 12 turquoise stripes on its lid and base and is copyrighted 1959. This Saccharin jar also comes in pink- and yellow-striped versions. Because of the vertical stripes, many novice collectors confuse this design with Holt-Howard's condiment jars. Value: $75-$85.

Horse radish: $95-$110 (from Dworkin Collection; photo by Van Blerck Photography).

HORSE RADISH

This Horse Radish is a very creative condiment jar by Davar. You can't help but smile once you notice the horse's head attached to a large radish. Beneath the horse's lid is an attached spoon. This piece stands 4-1/2 inches high and is 3 inches wide at its widest point. It's signed Davar, but not dated. Value: $95-$110.

Liquor decanters (Rye and Scotch): $45-$50 each (from Dworkin Collection; photo by Van Blerck Photography).

LIQUOR DECANTERS: RYE & SCOTCH

Although these Rye and Scotch are not pixies, they do share one Davar characteristic in common: handle-shaped arms. In the Davar pixies, the arms are flesh-colored; here on the decanters they are covered and decorated with clothing. The rye and scotch pictured above are both signed Davar Pro. (no date). Each decanter holds 2-1/2 cups of liquid and each has cork surrounding its stopper to seal tight its contents. Value: $45-$50 each.

Liquor decanter (rye): $45-$50 (from Dworkin Collection; photo by Van Blerck Photography).

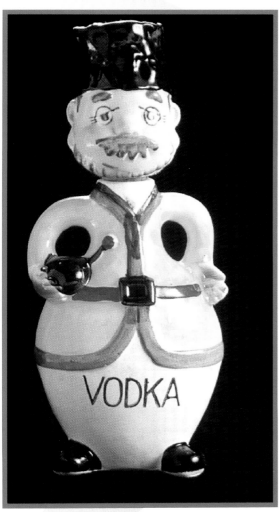

Liquor decanter (vodka): $45-$50 (from Dworkin Collection; photo by Van Blerck Photography).

LIQUOR DECANTER: VODKA

Due to his large Russian hat, this Vodka gentlemen stands about 1/2 inch taller than the rest of the decanters pictured here; however, all these decanters stand between 9 and 10 inches high. On the bottom of this piece, there is a blue and white sticker that reads "made in Japan." Although the vodka is not signed, one can't help but realize that it is part of the same series. Value: $45-$50.

LIQUOR DECANTER: RYE

The Rye decanter is the shortest of this group, barely measuring 9 inches high. This base is somewhat smaller than the other decanters and is only capable of holding 2 cups of libation. This piece is also not signed and has the same blue and white paper sticker as the vodka. Value $45-$50.

It should be noted that some of these liquor decanters have been showing up at flea markets and collectible shows with different paper labels from other novelty ceramics companies, leading us to believe that Davar may not have designed this entire line, but may have just been a distributor of these Japan-made items.

51

Fallen angel decanters: $40-$45 each (from Dworkin Collection; photo by Van Blerck Photography).

Fallen angel decanter, vodka: $40-$45 (from collection of and photo by Darline Comisky).

Fallen angel decanter, bourbon: $40-$45 (from collection of and photo by Darline Comisky).

LIQUOR DECANTERS: FALLEN ANGELS

These are very unique liquor decanters, in the respect that all of them represent "fallen angels," except one, "Agna Pura," who is praying for all of them. Each decanter stands 9 inches tall and can hold slightly more than 2 cups of liquid. These decanters are copyrighted Davar 1962. Value: $40-$45 each.

Medicine jars—$35-$45 each; (above, from Sharon Spielman Collection; photo by Mary Norman; right, photo by Evan Pazol).

MEDICINE BOTTLE SPRING HEADS

These fun characters are part of an apothecary set that consists of six whimsical members, all of whom appear to be perched on top of the cure for what ails them. Each stands 4-1/2 inches tall; the set is copyrighted 1959. Originally sold with storage rack. Value: $35-$45 per jar.

Lion King pin cushion/tape measure: $15-$23 (from Dworkin Collection; photo by Van Blerck Photography).

LION KING PIN CUSHION/TAPE MEASURE

This lion king is another example of Davar's giftware lines. He stands 6-1/4 inches tall and his crown serves as a pin cushion. The opening above his nose holds additional sewing tools and he is equipped with his own built-in pull-out tape measurer, located behind his left leg. Value $15-$23.

Pan and kettle napkin holder/salt & pepper: $30-$35 (from John Clay and Judy Shute Collection; photo by Van Blerck Photography).

PAN AND KETTLE NAPKIN HOLDER/SALT & PEPPER

There amorous frying pan and tea kettle salt-and-pepper shakers wink at each other while hanging onto their house-shaped napkin holder. The napkin holder stands 3-3/4 inches and has a foil sticker label that reads "Davar Originals Japan." Value: $30-$35.

Mom and pop napkin holder/salt & peppers: $30-$35 (from John Clay and Judy Shute Collection; photo by Van Blerck Photography).

MOM AND POP NAPKIN HOLDER/SALT & PEPPER

Mom and pop salt and pepper shakers are "hanging out," but hooked onto their yellow car napkin holder. The napkin holder stands 3-3/4 inches high and has a Davar foil sticker. Value: $30-$35.

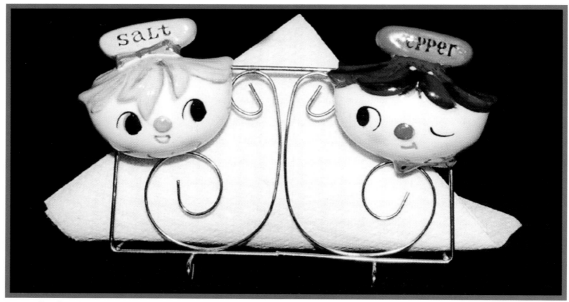

Boy and girl napkin holder/salt & peppers: $30-$35 (from the collection of and photo by Darline Comisky).

BOY AND GIRL NAPKIN HOLDER/SALT & PEPPER

The boy and girl salt and pepper set hook onto a brass napkin holder. This couple is reminiscent of Holt-Howard's Pixiewares because of the lettering on the tops of their heads and their pixie hairdos. This three-piece set is not signed but has the Davar foil sticker. Value: $30-$35.

Kitchen maids salt & peppers—$15-$20; spoon rest—$18-$23 (from John Clay and Judy Shute Collection; photo by Van Blerck Photography).

DAVAR KITCHEN MAIDS

The Davar kitchen maids salt and pepper set and matching spoon rest are copyrighted "Davar Products 1966." The shakers stand 4-3/4 inches high, and the spoon rest is 7 inches long. There are more matching pieces to the Davar Kitchen Maid Series, such as a soap-pad holder and other kitchen maids. Value: shaker set, $15-$20; spoon rest, $18-$23.

When the average consumer hears the name Lefton, the first picture that comes to mind is of fine china dinnerware and exclusive china patterns. But this very versatile company has also been manufacturing unique figurines and novelty collectibles for decades.

Georg Zoltan Lefton was founder of the present day Lefton Company, starting his own porcelain ceramics business in Chicago in 1941. After World War II, just like other ceramic and giftware companies of his time, Lefton sought out and established business relationships for manufacturing in Japan. Japan, because of its inexpensive cost of labor, was the ideal marketplace for manufacturing. Since this era, Lefton has created numerous all-occasion, every day and holiday-related collectibles. Lefton's line of Christmas items was always very extensive and highly collectible. Today, Lefton continues to be a family-run business and still stands strong as a major producer of ceramic giftwares and fine china throughout the world. The company has its main headquarters showrooms at 225 Fifth Ave., New York, and at numerous other showrooms through out the United States.

Lefton also joined the bandwagon to create condiment jars in the late 1950s and 1960s. The firm created an adorable line of fruit-, veggie- and human-headed jars. Lefton's large line of various condiment jars has vertical-striped bases, topped off with rounded fully dimensional heads. Lefton's jars have higher collars than Holt-Howard's

jars, and they are more cylindrical in appearance rather than rounded.

When compared to Holt-Howard, Lefton probably had the second largest selection of condiment jars to offer the general public, and it created more jars than the other numerous knock-off companies. The majority of Lefton's condiment jars are not signed by the company, but they are numbered in a black numeric series. Many years ago, all of these jars also had a red and silver foil label sticker which read "Lefton Reg. U.S. Pat. Off. Exclusives, Japan."

Also in this chapter are featured condiment jars that are signed "ESD Japan" that also have a black numeric identification series. ESD was a Canadian distributor that imported Lefton's jars into Canada. ESD was allocated a certain percentage of Lefton's jars for import from the manufacturing process in Japan, and the remaining balance would be imported to the United States.

Lefton's standard jar bottoms to this set measure 3-1/2 inches high and vary slightly in overall height according to the type of head closure they have. All jars have 13 vertical stripes that do not necessarily match or correspond in any manner with the color of their heads. This lack of color coordination between the tops and bottoms of these pieces can make it somewhat difficult for novice collectors to be assured they are purchasing the correct match; however, in some of these jars, their tops do give an indication of where they belong.

Ketchup: $55-$60 (from Dworkin Collection; photo by Van Blerck Photography).

KETCHUP

It's obvious that this ketchup head is a tomato showing off her tomato-leaf hairdo. In this jar, the pale red stripes match the color of her face. This piece stands 6 inches tall. Numeric identification: #1484. Value: $55-$60.

MUSTARDS

This is a very interesting pair. Time after time, these barbecue pals keep showing up in personal collections and at collectible shows with both heads as being the correct one for the base. Interestingly enough, the two pieces stare adoringly at each other and appear to be a pair! The hamburger bun head is wearing a pickle for a hat. Even though there is no presence of yellow in this adorable hotdog's head to match its stripes, you can't help but realize that no other condiment goes better with a hot dog than mustard! The hamburger head was featured in one of Lefton's catalogs on the mustard base,

Mustard with hamburger head: $80-$90 (from Dworkin Collection; photo by Van Blerck Photography).

Jam 'n jelly: $55-$60 (from Dworkin Collection; photo by Van Blerck Photography).

JAM 'N JELLY

This apple fruit head is colored predominately red with a green patch of color on the right side of her head; this red coloration matches perfectly with her jars' stripes. The Jam 'n Jelly stands 5-1/2 inches high. Numeric identification: #1485. Value: $55-$60.

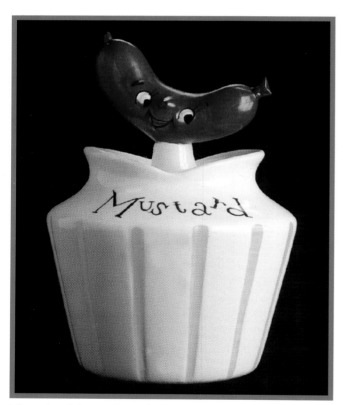

Mustard with hot-dog head: $80-$90 (from Dworkin Collection; photo by Van Blerck Photography).

but the hot dog was no where to be found! Unfortunately, there isn't sufficient historical records or catalogs which could help shed some light on this dilemma. We can only assume that this piece was issued twice with these different heads. Both pieces stand 5-1/2 inches tall. Numeric identification: #1482. Value: $80-$90 each.

Marmalade: $75-$85 (from Dworkin Collection; photo by Van Blerck Photography).

MARMALADE

It's not too often in the United States that we see marmalade condiment jars, since marmalade was more popular in England than here; however, this cute orange fruit head is an adorable companion to the Jam 'n Jelly.

The dark hunter-green stripes on this base do not match any of the coloration in its top; however, marmalade is made from oranges, so, of course, this is the correct match. If we include the upright leaf on her head, this marmalade miss stands 6 inches high. Numeric identification: #1483. Value: $75-$85.

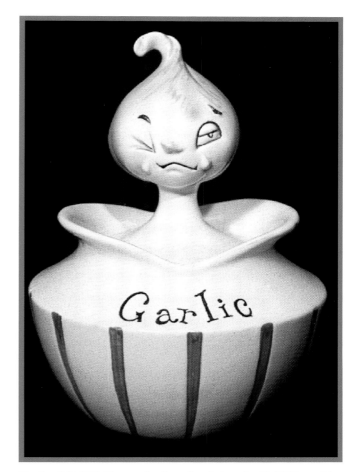

Garlic: $75-$85 (from collection of and photo by Hall/Glascock).

GARLIC

The garlic is a very interesting piece because this jar is shaped very differently than the rest of the Lefton clan. This piece is shorter than the others and only stands 5-1/4 inches high. Although the garlic jar is shaped differently, it still has 13 vertical maroon-colored stripes. These stripes compliment the pale shade of maroon on the top and back of its head. There isn't a spoon attached to this sad looking guy's head; instead, there is a cork liner around his lid to seal tight that overwhelming smell of garlic. Numeric identification: #1960. Value: $75-$85.

Relish: $75-$85 (from Dworkin Collection; photo by Van Blerck Photography).

RELISH JAR

Most collectors see this onion head and assume that it belongs on an onion or cocktail onion base; however, according to Lefton's catalog, the onion is the correct head for the relish jar. Since onion is a prime ingredient in the relish manufacturing process, it seems to make sense. This quite unhappy, tear-shedding condiment stands 6 inches tall, and the brown coloration in its head matches the brown stripes in its base. Numeric identification: #1481. Value: $75-$85.

COCKTAIL CHERRIES

The cocktail cherries and cocktail olives to this set are very unique—their jars' back sides are highly decorated with roosters and associated cocktail paraphernalia such as liquor bottles, shakers, glasses, lemon and limes and so on. Why the rooster? Supposedly, in England, rooster blood was added to drinks; hence, the name "cocktail" was born.

Notice that "Cocktail Cherries" is written on both

Cocktail cherries—front view: $75-$85 (from Dworkin Collection; photo by Van Blerck Photography).

Cocktail olives—front view: $75-$85 (from Dworkin Collection; photo by Van Blerck Photography).

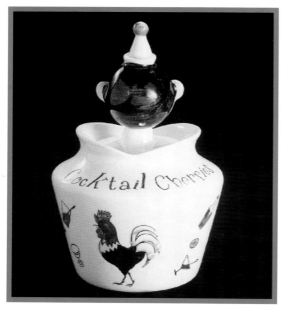

Cocktail cherries—back view (from Dworkin Collection; photo by Van Blerck Photography).

Cocktail olives—back view (from Dworkin Collection; photo by Van Blerck Photography).

the front and back of this piece. This is one of the few human-type heads that Lefton created. This crossed-eyed child wears a party hat and has a cherry in his mouth. At first glance, you sense a happy child's birthday party with lots of cherries available for ice cream sundaes, but...this is for cocktails! This piece has a hole in its spoon to drain juices and only has seven frontal red stripes. The container's stripes match the child's cherries in his mouth, on his nose and atop his head. Cocktail Cherries is 6-1/4 inches high and is signed ESD Japan. Numeric identification: #7858. Value: $75-$85.

COCKTAIL OLIVES

This winking olive head is showing off a pimento-stuffed olive in his mouth. He comes equipped with a hole in his spoon to drain liquids and has seven green frontal stripes that match the coloration of his head. The back side of this piece is also highly decorated, similar to the Cocktail Cherries, but different in design components. Pimento olives appear in the written description "Cocktail Olives" on front and back. This unique bar piece is 5-3/4 inches tall and is signed ESD Japan. Numeric identification: #7859. Value: $75-$85.

Cocktail olives and cocktail cherries: $95-$100 for pair (from Dworkin Collection; photo by Van Blerck Photography).

Instant coffee: $95-$110 (from Dworkin Collection; photo by Van Blerck Photography).

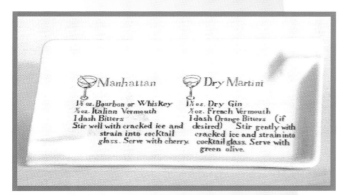

Tray for cocktail olives and cocktail cherries (from Sharon Spielman collection, photo by Evan Pazol).

COCKTAIL OLIVES AND CHERRIES

This adorable winking couple is much smaller than Lefton's other jars, each measuring a little more than 4 inches high. Both have 13 vertical stripes that match the coloration on the back portions of their heads. Although these jars don't have holes in their spoons, the spoons have scalloped edges to help drain juices. They come equipped with their own personalized bar tray/ash tray (7-3/4 x 4 inches), which has recipes for cocktails. Numeric identification (for all three pieces to this set): #1480. Value: $125 for complete set with tray.

INSTANT COFFEE

This instant coffee is very collectible, especially for collectors of black memorabilia. The cover to her lid is slightly smaller in diameter than other jars in this series and sits down lower in the jar's neck; hence, the piece seems to appear to have a higher collar above the jar's opening, but it's really the same as the others. Ms. Coffee wears a tropical flower in her hair and is equipped with a spoon. This piece has 13 coffee-brown stripes around the base with eight coffee beans pictured on the front of the jar. She stands 5-3/4 inches high and is signed ESD. Numeric identification: #7860. Value: $95-$110.

Coffee: $40-$50 (from Dworkin Collection; photo by Van Blerck Photography).

COFFEE

This coffee head, a "go along" with the instant coffee condiment jar, has the same face, flower and hairdo, but is also part of a two-piece coffee and tea set. Her lid has a cork around it to keep coffee air tight and fresh. She is in the shape of a coffee pot and her companion piece to the set is an oriental girl's head that reads "TEA" on top. This piece is 5 inches tall and is signed ESD. Numeric identification: #21728. Value: $40-$50.

Sugar & creamer: $65-$85 for set (from collection of and photo by Georgette Stock).

SUGAR & CREAMER

Sweet Lil' Sug is another small jar that only measures slightly more than 4 inches high and whose size is very similar to the small Lefton Cocktail Cherries and Olives. This cute sugar bowl has a built-in spoon and 13 blue stripes on her jar that match some of the coloration of the bow in her hair. She has a matching blue-striped 3-inch companion creamer piece "Lil' Cream Jug." Numeric identification: #1425. Value: $65-$85 for the set.

Salt & pepper: $35-$40 for pair (from Dworkin Collection; photo by Van Blerck Photography).

SALT & PEPPER

This girl's face on the salt shaker is very similar in appearance to the face on the Sweet Lil' Sug, and she is even licking her lips in a similar fashion. The little blonde boy is her pepper companion to the set. Each shaker has nine stripes on its base and measures about 4 inches high. Numeric identification (for pair): #1646. Value: $35-$40 for pair.

Sweetie syrup: $65-$75 (from Florence and Bill Bouma Collection; photo by Florence Bouma).

SYRUP

This Sweetie Syrup comes equipped with a built-in underplate to prevent drips. This little miss has 12 yellow stripes around her jug and matching yellow stripes on her underplate. The blonde-haired girl is licking her lips and bears the same resemblance to the head on the Lefton Sweet Lil' Sug. This piece measures 4-1/4 inches tall. Numeric identification: #1333. Value: $65-$75.

Oil & vinegar: $95-$110 each (from Dworkin collection; photo by Van Blerck Photography).

OIL & VINEGAR

This oil and vinegar set is a wonderful compliment to the Lefton collection. The shapes and style of their jars are very unique. The olive head seems very content and flirtatious, while his lemon head companion seems to be frowning (perhaps due to the vinegar that she is concealing). The olive most likely represents olive oil while the lemon represents the sourness of vinegar. The novice collector can always identify the correct heads for this pair since the olive's red bow tie and pimento hat match his 11 stripes, and the lemon's hunter-green necklace matches her jar's 11 stripes. Each piece stands about 9 inches tall and comes equipped with a plastic pouring spout inside that is surrounded by cork to prevent spillage. Each cruet can hold 1-1/3 cups of liquid. Numeric identification (both pieces): #1334. Value: $95-$110 each.

DRESSING JARS

Lefton created three dressing cruets: Russian, French and Italian. The three jars are very individualistic and well decorated. Although there are many differences in their styling, the one characteristic that they all have in common is that each one is holding vegetables for the preparation of salads. Each cruet jar holds 2 cups of liquids. The Russian dressing differs greatly in that its base doesn't have stripes like the French and Italian cruets. Numeric identifications: French—#2089; Russian—#2090; Italian—#2091. Value: $95-$110 each.

French dressing: $95-$110 (from collection of and photo by Hall/Glascock).

Italian dressing: $95-$110 (from collection of and photo by Hall/Glascock).

Russian dressing: $95-$110 (from collection of and photo by Hall/Glascock).

MR. & MRS. CLAUS JAM 'N JELLY & RELISH

Evidently, Lefton's condiment jars were so successful that the company decided to carry this design theme into its Christmas giftware line. Here Mr. & Mrs. Claus stare lovingly at each other and wear an identical Santa cap. Both stand 6 inches tall and have 13 red stripes around their jars. Numeric identifications: Santa—#1651; Mrs. Claus—#1652. Value: $55-65 each.

Mr. & Mrs. Claus jam 'n jelly and relish: $55-$65 each (from Dworkin Collection; photo by Van Blerck Photography).

Sweet Santa & Lil' Cream jug: $75-$85 for pair (from Dworkin Collection; photo by Van Blerck Photography).

SWEET SANTA & LIL' CREAM JUG

As part of this Christmas set, we see a Sweet Santa which is a miniature version of the Jam 'n Jelly Santa, except that this Santa is staring upwards rather than to the side. He is only 4-1/2 inches high. This piece comes equipped with his own personalized Lil' Cream Jug which stands 3 inches high. This creamer has 12 red stripes, while its matching sugar bowl has 13. Numeric identification (both items): #1650. Value: $75-$85 for the pair.

MR. AND MRS. CLAUS OIL AND VINEGAR

This Lefton Santa set also came with a matching Mr. and Mrs. Claus oil and vinegar couple whose bases are identical in structure to the lemon-and-lime-headed oil-and-vinegar cruet set pictured on page 60. The Christmas oil-and-vinegar pieces have red stripes, and their heads are identical in appearance to the Mr. and Mrs. Claus heads that appear on the Jam 'n Jelly and Relish. Numeric identification (both items): #1653. Value: $95-$110 each.

This chapter is dedicated to condiment jar girls that either have floral-or polka dot-designed bases. They were all created around the same time-frame, and many sets share some common traits. This first collection, created by L&M, not only has floral bases, but the girls also have beautiful large flowers that surround and decorate their heads.

LIPPER & MANN FLOWER GIRLS

The Lipper & Mann (L&M) novelty ceramic company was started in 1949 by business partners Seymour Mann and Hal Lipper. This novelty ceramics business was located in New York; by the mid 1960s, the name of the business was changed to Lipper International when Seymour Mann left the partnership. Lipper International is still in business today and located in Wallingford, Connecticut, and run by President Amy Lipper. This company has its main showroom located at 225 Fifth Ave., New York City.

L&M created the "Flower Girls" condiment jars. All the pieces to this set are girls that have similar bases which are white and decorated with small green six-petaled daisies. The notable differences in the designs of these condiment girls are the many different types of beautiful flowers that decorate their heads. The unique flowers completely surround the girls' faces and serve as large bonnets that cover the backs of their heads completely. Underneath these flowers is a wide array of different hairdos that give each girl individuality.

L&M flower girls are not signed; however, they all have red ink stamp identification numbers under their bases and a red and gold foil sticker (shaped like a condiment jar) that reads "Lipper & Mann creations Japan." Most of the condiment jars in this series have the exact same numbers on their bases—23/71. Evidently, L&M used the same identification numbers on all bases of the same physical design, even though the condiment names written on the fronts of these jars were all different.

Some of the pieces to this set appear to have been issued twice, with two completely different heads and different colored flowers. Examples of this duplication are the salts and peppers and instant coffee jars.

Mustard and ketchup: $65-$75 each (from Dworkin Collection; photo by Van Blerck Photography).

L&M: MUSTARD & KETCHUP

Ms. Mustard has a four-petaled yellow flower for a bonnet, while her companion ketchup wears a seven-petaled pink flower. These sisters stand 6-1/2 inches tall and have built-in spoons to scoop out the mustard and ketchup. Both are numbered 23/71. Value: $65-$75 each.

Jam 'n jelly: $65-$75 (from Dworkin Collection; photo by Van Blerck Photography).

L&M: JAM 'N JELLY

Ms. Jam 'n Jelly sports a five-petaled purple flower on her head, which is typical of her condiment jar sisters. She has 15 daisies that decorate her base. This piece is numbered 23/71. Value: $65-$75.

Relish: $75-$80 (from Dworkin Collection; photo by Van Blerck Photography).

L&M: RELISH JAR

Our relish girl wears a seven-petaled blue flower bonnet and is numbered 23/71. Value: $75-$80.

Instant coffee jars: $95-$100 each (from Dworkin Collection; photo by Van Blerck Photography).

L&M: INSTANT COFFEES

The proof of duplication in the Flower Girls series is very evident here as we examine the two instant coffee jars. These are specially designed heads with cork surrounding the bases of their lids to seal coffee freshness. These heads are not compatible with any other pieces to this set and will only fit the coffee bases. This duo is structured somewhat differently from their sisters, and since they don't have a spoon under their lids, they come equipped with a built in spoon holder on their sides. These sisters are a little larger than the rest of their family and stand 7 inches tall. Each piece is numbered 23/73. Value: $95-$100 each.

Two sets of salt & peppers: $55-$60 per set (from Dworkin Collection; photo by Van Blerck Photography).

L&M: SALT & PEPPERS

These two sets of salts & peppers are conclusive proof that two versions of some of the pieces to this set were manufactured. Each pair of these cuties stare at their companion and each shaker stands 5-3/4 inches tall. Notice how similar the purple and yellow shakers are to the oil & vinegar set, while the blue and pink shakers have a strong resemblance to the ketchup and relish jars. These pieces are the only ones to the set that have green leaves decorating their bottoms. Notice how different the ribbed-leaf structure is on the pink pepper compared to the smooth edge leaves of the other three shakers.

These two sets are very unique in that, although similar, there are notable differences. Three of the four girls wear necklaces similar to the oil & vinegar, while the blue flower salt hasn't any necklace at all! Perhaps her extra long hair would only cover the necklace. The pink-flowered pepper's necklace is twice as long as the ones of her purple and yellow sisters. All shakers have seven green daisies that adorn their bases and all four are numbered 23/70, even though we see many differences in their make-ups. Value: $55-$60 per set.

Cream & sugar: $65-$85 for set (from Dworkin Collection; photo by Van Blerck Photography).

L&M: Cream & Sugar

The cream & sugar set appear quite miniature in stature compared to the rest of this set. The sugar measures 5 inches high. The creamer holds a half cup of liquid, is barely 3 inches high (at top of head), 2-3/4 inches wide and 3-1/2 inches long. Ms. Sugar licks her sweet lips, while her companion creamer just smiles. I've only seen two of these sugars; in both pieces, neither one had an attached spoon. Both pieces have 12 green daisies decorating their bases. The sugar is not numbered and the creamer is marked 23/74. Value: $65-$85 for the set.

Floral- & Polka Dot-Skirted Girls

In the following section, I have grouped together three sets of little girl condiment jars because so many collectors are confusing the sets. The girls in these sets all wear bows in their hair and either have floral or polka dotted dresses. Collectors are not only mixing up these sets, but are also confusing many of these pieces with Holt-Howard's Pixiewares. Even though these three sets aren't pixies, nor do they have any stripes on their jars, collectors see the bows in the girl's hair and automatically form an immediate association with Holt-Howard's Pixieware line (such as the instant coffee and Lil' sugar).

Oil & vinegar: $95-$100 each (from Dworkin Collection; photo by Van Blerck Photography).

L&M: Oil & Vinegar

These Oil & Vinegar girls stand 8 inches tall and come equipped with corks under their lids to seal in their contents and prevent spillage. Both jars are capable of holding one cup of liquid. Each cruet has the 15 green daisies decorating its base and each girl's neck is adorned with a white beaded necklace. Both pieces are numbered 23/72. Value: $95-$100 each.

Jolly Floral Girls

For all practical purposes in this text, I would like to refer to this first set as the "Jolly Floral Girls," since they never turn up with a signature or manufacturer's label. To date, all efforts to identify the company that created and manufactured this set of little girls has failed. Many collectors have these pieces and all we have in common to identify them is a blue rectangular paper sticker with white lettering that reads "Japan." I once attended a major collectibles show and was fortunate enough to find the salt & pepper set in mint condition in its original box; however, all that was printed on the box cover was "Jolly" salt & pepper set, and the enclosed shakers still didn't have any signature or paper sticker, except for the label that reads "Japan."

The Jolly Floral Girls not only have the same Holt-Howard-style bows in their hair, but are also confusing to the novice collector since they have similar pixie-shaped top knots and protruding ears. Upon close examination, you can't help but notice that these cuties are definitely not pixies, but are little girls. They don't have pixie hairdos and should not be confused with pixies. Jolly Floral Girls seem to share the same type hairdos, similar dresses and a close family resemblance to each other. Upon close examination, you will notice that they all have different shaped eyes; also, while some lick their lips in sweet delight, others hardly give us a smile. When purchasing Jolly Floral Girls, the novice collector should always make sure that the color of the bow in the girl's hair matches her shoes and the flowers on her dress; this will ensure the correct head is on the matching base.

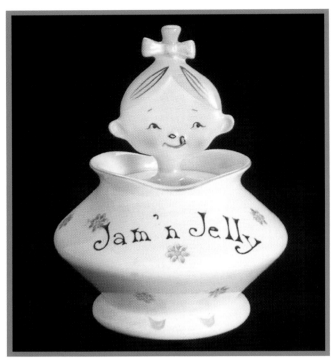

Jolly jam 'n jelly: $65-$75 (from Dworkin Collection; photo by Van Blerck Photography).

Jolly mustard and ketchup: $65-$75 each. (from Dworkin Collection; photo by Van Blerck Photography).

JOLLY MUSTARD & KETCHUP

Most knock-off companies that manufactured limited condiment pieces in their collections would start off with a mustard and ketchup and expand into a jam and jelly or relish (since they were the most widely used pieces). To date, this set appears to have only encompassed a line of four condiments, including a salt & pepper set. The Jolly Floral Girls have 15 daisy flowers adorning their dresses, which are color-coordinated to match their bows, shoes and rim line around their jar's collar. All four condiment's come with a spoon attached to serve up their jar's contents; however, the mustard has a spreader rather than a spoon. Value: $65-$75 each.

Jolly relish: $75-$90 (from Deanna and Gale Longnecker Collection; photo by Van Blerck Photography).

JOLLY JAM 'N JELLY & RELISH

This jam 'n jelly and relish, along with the mustard and ketchup, each stand 5-1/2 inches tall. Value: Jam 'n Jelly—$65-$75; Relish—$75-$90.

Jolly salt & pepper: $40-$45 for set (from Dworkin Collection; photo by Van Blerck Photography).

JOLLY SALT & PEPPER

This salt appears quite happy, while her companion piece seems to be somewhat annoyed from having to deal with all that pepper! An interesting design feature about this twosome is that both shakers have the same amount of holes to pour out their contents (located behind their necks). The salt's three holes are much larger than the pepper's. Each piece is decorated with six daisy-type flowers on their dresses which match the bows in their hair. Each shaker stands 5 inches tall. Value: $40-$45.

Mustard and ketchup: $65-$75 each (from Dworkin Collection; photo by Van Blerck Photography).

M-G: MUSTARD & KETCHUP

This adorable set of polka-dotted skirted girls was created by M-G Inc. All pieces in this set are girls with bows in their hair (the color of their bows always matches the polka dots on their dresses and the collar ring around the jar's opening). The color of their hair always matches the three bottom horizontal stripes that adorn their dresses.

This set was copyrighted in 1960; unfortunately, only some of these pieces are signed and dated and the rest may only have a green and silver foil sticker which reads " M.G. Japan." All these little misses have flesh-colored faces and always have their two arms extended over their stomachs.

The Mustard and Ketchup stare at each other with blue eyes that have very large black pupils (typical of this set). Ms. Mustard licks her lips while her companion ketchup smiles with an open mouth. Both have spreader-type spoons attached underneath their lids. This duo stands 5 inches high. Value: $65-$75 each.

Jam 'n jelly and relish: $65-$75 each (from Dworkin Collection; photo by Van Blerck Photography).

M-G: JAM 'N JELLY AND RELISH

Ms. Jam 'n Jelly licks her lips and has 13 polka dots that adorn her dress (typical of all these pieces). Notice her blond hair matches the color of the stripes around the bottom of her dress. Ms. Relish adds a wonderful color contrast to this set, with the introduction of purple fashion. These two pieces have standard-shaped spoons (rather than spreaders) attached to their lids. Both are 5 inches tall. Value: $65-$75 each.

Cream & sugar: $140-$150 for pair (from Dworkin Collection; photo by Van Blerck Photography).

M-G: CREAM & SUGAR

This set is a real eye-catcher. The pair stares at each other and are large enough to service a lot of desert guests. Ms. Cream can hold one cup of liquid and comes equipped with her own pouring handle in back of her dress. Ms. Sugar has a built-in spoon. Both pieces are 5 inches tall. Value: $140-$150 for the pair.

Match holder: $85-$90 (from Dworkin Collection; photo by Van Blerck Photography).

M-G: MATCH HOLDER

Ms. Match Holder is a real novelty and a unique kitchen piece especially designed to hold wooden matches to light the stove. She is a taller than her other M-G sisters at 5-1/4 inches tall. This piece has three yellow stripes on her dress (on either side of match holder) that match the color of her hair. Ms. Match Holder was also issued in a lavender color scheme. Value: $85-$90.

Saccharin: $65-$75 (from Dworkin Collection; photo by Van Blerck Photography).

M-G: SACCHARIN

Compared to the other novelty condiment and other jars, Ms. Saccharin is a true miniature at only 3 inches high. This piece also has a tiny built-in spoon to scoop out the saccharin. Value: $65-$75.

Salt & pepper: $35-$45 for set (from Dworkin Collection; photo by Van Blerck Photography).

M-G: SALT & PEPPER

As we examine the entire M-G set, we notice that in most of the pieces that are paired together, one little miss is always licking her lips, while the other has an open mouth and is smiling. These same characteristics are evident in the salt and pepper set. This duo stares at each other and is 4 inches high. The pepper has three small pouring holes behind her shoulders, while the salt has two larger holes. Value: $35-$45.

Ketchup, mustard and relish: $65-$75 each (from Dworkin Collection; photo by Van Blerck Photography).

NORCREST: KETCHUP, MUSTARD & RELISH

The Norcrest China Company was started in 1917 in Portland, Oregon, by Hide Naito; at that time, the business was called "The H. Naito Company." After World War II, the company branched out into two businesses and changed its name to Norcrest China Company and Pacific Orient Company. The two companies were importing and distributing novelty ceramics in United States and Canada. Eventually, Pacific Orient was absorbed into Norcrest China. Norcrest China has survived for more than 70 years and is still in business today in Portland. It issues catalogs twice a year and has offered huge selections of holiday, kitchen and numerous other novelty collectibles and tableware accessories.

Everyone who sees this set by Norcrest falls in love with it. The girls all have two ribbons in their hair that match the color of the daisy type flowers on their dresses.

Each base is decorated with 17 flowers, and two more flowers appear on the lid at either side of the girl's necks. Reliable sources claim there is a fourth sister—Jam 'n Jelly.

These girls don't have spoons attached to their lids; instead, special oval openings are located in the back of their lids for the insertion of a plastic spoon (4-1/2 inches long) to scoop out their contents. These sisters display their left arms over their stomach in a similar fashion as the M-G girls; however, their right arms are elevated and opened to serve as holders for their spoons.

This set is not signed, but is numbered (relish is #J-488, mustard is #J-489 and ketchup is #J-490). All three pieces have a green and gold foil sticker that says "Reg. US Pat. Off. Norcrest Japan." This cheerful trio is larger than most other sets at 5-3/4 inches tall. Value: $65-$75 each.

In this chapter, we are going to examine more condiment jars and related novelty items. All these collectibles fall into the category of "Others Made In Japan." First, we are going to see condiment jars that are similar in construction to Holt-Howard's Pixiewares line. Many of these jars are not signed; unfortunately, to this day, many still remain anonymous. We'll also see many of Napcoware's ceramic condiments which are numbered on their bases or at least have the company's well-known silver foil sticker to identify them. Secondly, we're going to explore the full-headed condiment jars that are completely different from Pixiewares. Although these full-headed jars are different in design, they were contemporaries of Pixiewares and other condiment jars that were all competing for sales on store shelves during the late 1950s and early 1960s. Condiment jars, such as those manufactured by the DeForest Company of California, may have been issued two years earlier than the Pixiewares. This chapter will also help identify a few more kitchen and bar-related novelties that are either Holt-Howard look-a-likes or related to other collectibles in this book.

Betson mustard & ketchup: $60-$65 each (from Dworkin Collection; photo by Van Blerck Photography).

BETSON MUSTARD AND KETCHUP

From what I've seen of this set, all its members seem to be round fruit heads. The entire family appears to be happy-go-lucky except for our mustard guy pictured here, who, like many other mustards, seems upset. None of the pieces to this set are signed; however, some are ink stamped "Japan," while others just have a blue and white rectangular paper sticker that reads "Japan." One piece has finally turned up with a clue to our manufacturer, with a blue paper sticker that reads "Betson." All members of this collection measure 5-1/2 inches high and have a built-in spoon under their lids. One shared design characteristic is that the color of their heads is always coordinated to match the color of their two buttons and the lower part of their base. Value: $60-$65 each.

BETSON JAM 'N JELLY JARS

It's amazing that Betson created so many (three) jam 'n jellies plus a marmalade jar! At first glance, you would almost think that these two jars are the same; however, one is obviously a pear head, while the

companion piece appears to be a yellow apple. Value: $60-$65 each.

Betson jam 'n jelly jars: $60-$65 each (from Dworkin Collection; photo by Van Blerck Photography).

Betson strawberry jam and marmalade: $60-$65 each (from Dworkin Collection; photo by Van Blerck Photography).

BETSON STRAWBERRY JAM AND MARMALADE JARS

Another two Betson jars: one is a strawberry jam jar; the other is a grape-colored marmalade jar. Value: $60-$65 each.

Chefs ketchup and mustard: $35-$40 each (from Dworkin Collection; photo by Van Blerck Photography).

Chefs jam 'n jelly and relish: $35-$40 each (from Dworkin Collection; photo by Van Blerck Photography).

THE CHEFS (UNIDENTIFIED)

I've always called this set "The Chefs" because of the chef hats on all the pieces. Many collectors call the blond-haired girls "Campbell's Soup Kids look-a-likes." The nice part about this set is their gaily colored plaid bases. Since most of these thick flat heads are alike, there isn't any insurance about matching up the correct head with the right base. The males are identical with black bow ties, as are the females with yellow necklaces on their necks. The males have always shown up on the Ketchup and Relish jars, while the girls have always shown up on the Jam 'n Jelly and Mustard. These pieces stand 5 inches high and have very narrow spoons attached under their lids. The pieces are not signed and only have a white paper sticker with black letters that reads "Japan." Value: $35-$40 each.

Blondies ketchup, mustard & relish: $40-$45 each (from Dworkin Collection; photo by Van Blerck Photography).

THE BLONDIES (UNIDENTIFIED)

I've always called this set "The Blondies." Each little round-headed girl has blond hair with a blue bow

and stands 5 inches tall. Although all the girls are crossed eyed, the mustard has shown up once not crossed eyed and looking to her right side (perhaps a factory error?). Even though all the girls look identical, each piece's lid is decorated around its edges with the same color to match the eight vertical stripes on its base. These girls all have arm handles similar to the Davar pixies and narrow spoons similar in construction to "The Chefs" condiment jars. Value: $40-$45 each.

Swirl girls round-headed mustard and Jam 'n Jelly: $65-$75 each (from Dworkin Collection; photo by Van Blerck Photography).

Swirl girls flat-headed ketchup and cherry: $65-$75 each (from Dworkin Collection; photo by Van Blerck Photography).

SWIRL GIRLS KETCHUP, MUSTARD, JAM 'N JELLY AND CHERRY (UNIDENTIFIED)

This unidentified series is very bizarre, for they were evidently manufactured in a flat-headed and round-headed series. The flat-headed girls have pixie-type hairdos and ears, while the round headed ones do not! The construction of the jars and built-in spoons are identical on both the flat and round heads. Each jar has eight swirled stripes. The round blond headed Jam 'n Jelly face bears a very strong resemblance to the Lefton "Lil' sugar" and "Sweetie Syrup." These pieces are not signed, except for the words "Japan" on their bottoms. Value: $65-$75.

FOUR MUSTACHE GUYS (UNIDENTIFIED)

These four gents are very colorful and stand 5-1/4 inches high. They all share a pink bow-tie in common and a blue and silver foil label sticker which reads "Exclusive BP Japan." Our mustard and relish jars share the same head, which leads me to believe that one jar may possibly not have the correct lid! Value: $50-$60 each.

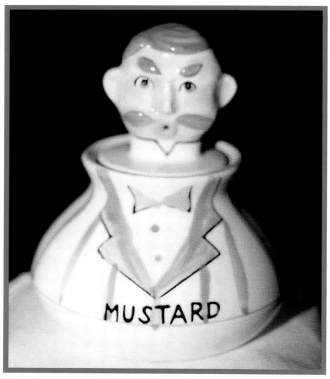

Mustache guy mustard: $50-$60 (from collection of Florence and Bill Bouma; photo by Florence Bouma).

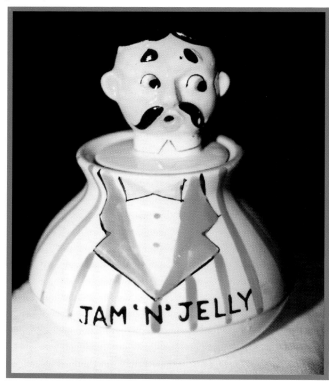

Mustache guy Jam 'n Jelly: $50-$60 (from collection of Florence and Bill Bouma; photo by Florence Bouma).

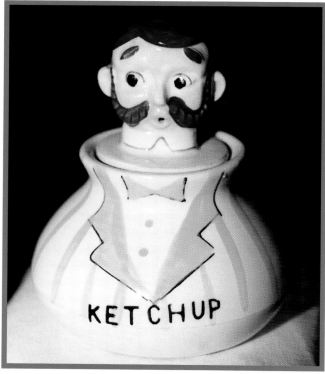

Mustache guy ketchup: $50-$60 (from collection of Florence and Bill Bouma; photo by Florence Bouma).

Mustache guy relish: $50-$60 (from collection of Florence and Bill Bouma; photo by Florence Bouma).

Unsigned jam lady: $45-$55 (from collection of Florence and Bill Bouma; photo by Florence Bouma).

Napco ketchup and onions: $65-$75 each (from Dworkin Collection; photo by Van Blerck Photography).

Unsigned jam 'n jelly guy: $45-$55 (from collection of Florence and Bill Bouma; photo by Florence Bouma).

JAM AND JELLIES CONDIMENT JARS (UNIDENTIFIED)

This jam lady (pictured at top) has five horizontal pink stripes and smiles as she licks her lips. She stands 6-1/2 inches tall. The Jam 'n Jelly fellow (pictured above) appears to have a Pixieware-type hairdo and lettering atop his head similar to the Pixieware liquor bottles. He also has arms similar to the Davar pixies and stands 5-1/4 inches high. Unfortunately, neither of these pieces are signed. Value: $45-$55 each.

NAPCO KETCHUP AND ONIONS

This very popular family-owned novelty ceramics company was started up during the late 1930s. Napco stands for National Potteries Company of Cleveland, Ohio. Napco was an importing, as well as a distributing, company. It dealt in a wide variety of adorable novelty ceramics from Japan, including figural items, salt and pepper shakers, planters, banks, liquor decanters and other holiday-related products. Napco was especially well known for its huge Christmas product lines. Napco usually used alpha/numeric letters to identify its products, accompanied with a silver foil sticker shaped like an artist's palette which read "National Potteries Co. Cleveland/Made in Japan." Sometimes, just the letter "N" with a circle around it or just the letter "c" with a circle around it for copyright (plus the Napco name) would appear stamped on the base of a ceramic piece.

In 1960, a relative of the family started up another company called Inarco and both Napco and Inarco produced separate lines of novelty ceramics. In 1991, Napco and Inarco merged to handle the same product lines, resulting in a new company named "LBK," which is still flourishing today, producing beautiful ceramics with its headquarters located in Jacksonville, Florida. These ketchup and onion jars (pictured above) are two examples of Napco's condiment jars, identified easily by their charcoal and pink plaid-striped bases. Each piece comes with a built-in spoon and stands 5 inches high. The ketchup is signed with numbers "K 3948" and the onions has "K 3949." Value: $65-$75.

Napco human head mustard: $65-$75 (from collection of Deanna and Gale Longnecker; photo by Van Blerck Photography).

NAPCO HUMAN HEAD MUSTARD

Why Napco intermixed a human head along with their vegetable head series is a mystery. At first, when I saw this piece, I thought it was a mismatch; however, this piece has turned up numerous times with the same human head! It stands 5-1/4 inches high is numbered "K3947." Value: $65-$75.

Napco jam and mustard: $35-$45 each (from Dworkin Collection; photo by Van Blerck Photography).

NAPCO MUSTARD AND JAM

In addition to creating the previously mentioned condiment jars, Napco also created a line of full-headed-type jars with large hats that spelled out their jar's contents. The mustard jar stands 4-1/4 inches tall and has the silver Napco foil sticker and number "K2597" on its bottom. The jam jar stands 4-3/4 inches tall with the same sticker and is numbered "K2596." Value: $35-$45.

Napco relish: $35-$45 (from Dworkin Collection; photo by Van Blerck Photography).

NAPCO RELISH

This relish is very different in appearance with her squashed down face and flat hat; and isn't that a serving of relish on top of her hat? This piece is 3-1/2 inches high, has the silver Napco foil sticker and is numbered "K2595." The Napco mustard, jam and relish all have an opening on the side of their heads for the insertion of a spoon. Value: $35-$45.

Napco may-o-naise and onion: $35-$45 each (from Dworkin Collection; photo by Van Blerck Photography).

NAPCO ONIONS AND MAY O'NAISE

This sad looking but colorful onion fellow appears a little shorter than the rest of his Napco cousins, but, with his high pointed lid, he actually is 4-1/2 inches high. His head is fluted all around and he truly looks like an onion. This piece also has an opening on its side for a spoon and is numbered "K2967." The Napco May O'Naise bears a very strong resemblance to the DeForest May O'Naise. This smiling lady stands 4-1/4 inches and has the same opening for a spoon on the side of her head. May O'Naise is numbered "K2968." Value: $35-$45 each.

Napco salt & pepper: $12-$18 for set (from Dworkin Collection; photo by Van Blerck Photography).

NAPCO YELLOW HAT SALT AND PEPPER SHAKERS

This salt-and-pepper shaker set is definitely go-along with Napco's full-headed condiment jars. The pair is not signed; however, both are numbered "1818" which could represent Napco as the manufacturer. The pair stands 3-1/4 inches high. Value: $12-$18 for set.

DeForest jam, mustard and mayonnaise: $35-$45 each (from Dworkin Collection; photo by Van Blerck Photography).

DEFOREST JAM, MUSTARD AND MAYONNAISE

DeForest was a California-based business that operated from 1950 through 1970. The company was a family-run business, founded by Margaret and Jack De Forest and their sons, with Jack DeForest serving as the corporation's president. DeForest and Napco created similar full-headed condiment jars; sometimes it's hard to differentiate between the two competing companies' product lines. All the DeForest condiment jars represented in this chapter are signed "DeForest of California Hand Painted." Interestingly enough, some of them may have been released two years before Pixiewares. Some of these DeForest pieces have a copyright "C" on the rear base of their heads, which seems to be accompanied with a date such as 1956 or 1958. DeForest not only created human-type but also vegetable, herb, cheese and other whimsical heads.

These are three of DeForest's human type heads: Jam, Mustard and May O'Naise. All three pieces have openings on the sides of their heads for the insertion of

a spoon. On the backs of their heads, the Jam has a "C '56" and May O'Naise has "C 1957." Our mustard guy only has a "C" and no date. Value: $35-$45 each.

DeForest Pat O' Dip—$45-$55; Bar-B-Q sauce with spoon—$75-$85 (from collection of and photo by Evan Pazol).

DEFOREST PAT O'DIP AND BAR-B-Q SAUCE

These two rosy cheeked smiling party helpers are named Pat O'Dip and Bar-B-Q Sauce. Bar-B-Q Sauce has an opening in its lid to accommodate its original hefty-sized spoon. Pat O'Dip and Bar-B-Q Sauce are two of the less common DeForest pieces. Value: DeForest Pat O'Dip—$45-$55; Bar-B-Q Sauce with spoon—$75-$85.

DeForest Mr. & Mrs. Garlic: $45-$50 (from Dworkin Collection; photo by Van Blerck Photography).

DEFOREST MR. & MRS. GARLIC

This happy and sad couple, Mr. & Mrs. Garlic, is 4-1/2 inches high and decorated with garlic leaves around its base. There's a small air exchange hole in its lid to allow for a fresh air flow to keep garlic cloves fresh. Value: $45-$50.

DeForest onions and garlic: $35-$45 each (from Dworkin Collection; photo by Van Blerck Photography).

DeForest Onions and Garlic

This DeForest Onions and Garlic jars are about 4-3/4 inches tall. The back of the onions has a "C" with no date, while the garlic has a "C 1956." Neither piece has an opening for a spoon—a clever design that keeps the jar sealed tight so the odors of garlic and onion will not escape. Value: $35-$45 each.

DeForest big cheese and big cheese slice: $35-$45 each (from Dworkin Collection; photo by Van Blerck Photography).

DeForest Big Cheese and Big Cheese slice

DeForest Big Cheese has a "C 1956" behind its head and a large hat to seal-in odors. Big Cheese is 4-1/2 inches high. Big Cheese slice is 4-3/4 inches high and has an opening on its side for the insertion of a spoon. Value: $35-$45 each.

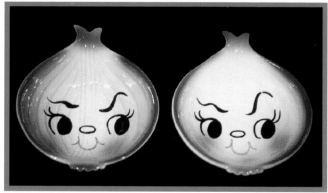

DeForest onion plates: $18-$22 each (from Sharon Spielman Collection; photo by Mary Norman).

DeForest Onion Plates

This pair of smiling, but mischievous-looking, onion plates, were sold with more matching pieces, including salt-and-pepper shakers, a soup tureen coffee mugs and a four-piece canister set. Value (plates): $18-$22 each.

DeForest Horace Radish and relish: $45-$50 each (from Dworkin Collection; photo by Van Blerck Photography).

DeForest Hamburger Head Relish & Horace Radish

This cute Relish jar truly resembles a hamburger, with its two buns, relish oozing out of its burger and topped off with a pimento olive on its head. The DeForest hamburger head is 3-1/2 inches tall and has a "C '56" behind its head. Horace Radish wears a great derby hat that covers his green hair. His whimsical name represents horse radish, which is not common in the world of condiment jars. Value: $45-$50 each.

Unsigned crying onion with pointed head: $35-$45 (from Dworkin Collection; photo by Van Blerck Photography).

Crying Onion with Pointed Head (unsigned)

This crying onion is 5 inches high and is not signed. Value: $35-$45.

American Bisque relish and jam: $50-$60 each (from Dworkin Collection; photo by Van Blerck Photography).

AMERICAN BISQUE RELISH AND JAM

American Bisque was well known for its kitchen-related ceramics, such as condiment jars, salt-and-pepper shakers, cookie jars, planters and so on. The company manufactured on a large scale, not only for itself, but for other distributors, also. This novelty pottery company was founded in 1919 in Williamstown, West Virginia, and went out of business during the mid 1980s. American Bisque also created a line of full-headed condiment jars. These pieces can be easily confused with its competition. These gentlemen are a little larger than other companies', with the jam standing at 5-3/4 inches high, and the relish at 5 inches. Both pieces have openings in the back of their heads to accommodate a spoon. Although these pieces are not signed, they are believed to be manufactured by American Bisque, possibly issued under the Cardinal Company label. Value: $50-$60 each.

American Bisque onions and jam: $50-$60 each (from Lori Smith Collection; photo by Van Blerck Photography).

AMERICAN BISQUE ONIONS AND JAM

These two condiments are not signed; however, they are also believed to have been manufactured by American Bisque and also possibly distributed by Cardinal. Both the sad-faced onion clown and freckled-faced girl have counterpart cookie jars that resemble

them exactly. The onion clown stands 5-1/2 inches high; the freckle-faced girl wears a blue bow in the back of her hair and is 5 inches tall. Both pieces also have openings behind their heads to accommodate a spoon. Value: $50-$60 each.

Lego egg cup couples: $35-$45 each (from Dworkin Collection; photo by Van Blerck Photography).

LEGO EGG CUP COUPLES

These smiling couples were created by the Lego Company and are shaped like large egg cups. The guys wear yellow hats and the girls wear green. The couples stare at each other and appear to be the ideal mates. It's apparent that a guy and girl were created for each of the four condiments: Jam 'n Jelly, Mustard, Ketchup and Relish. All of these condiments have openings on the side of their hats to accommodate spoons. This is quite a family reunion, since these pieces were all found in different states of the country. "Hail, hail the gang's all here," except for our lady Ketchup with a green hat! All stand 5 inches high and are signed "Lego 1959," accompanied by a red and silver foil sticker which reads "Fine Quality Lego Japan." Value: $35-$45 each.

Lego cigarette holders/ashtray: $25-$35 each (from Dworkin Collection; photo by Van Blerck Photography).

LEGO CIGARETTE HOLDERS/ASHTRAY

This Lego couple is smaller than the condiment jars (about 4 inches high) and appear to be cigarette holders, since the reverse side of their hats are ashtrays and spell out "ashes." Also, there is an even smaller salt-and-pepper set that matches this series. Value: $25-$35 each.

Commodore mustard and ketchup: $30-$35 each (from Dworkin Collection; photo by Van Blerck Photography).

COMMODORE MUSTARD AND KETCHUP

This Mustard and Ketchup set of two little girls was created by the Commodore Company. Their pointed hairdos and bows, plus the mustard's peevish facial expression, are very reminiscent of Holt-Howard's Pixiewares. Each girl is 4-3/4 inches high and has a built-in spoon attached underneath her lid. Value: $30-$35 each.

Cherry n' lemon: $35-$45 (from Dworkin Collection; photo by Van Blerck Photography).

CHERRY N' LEMON (UNSIGNED)

This Cherry n' Lemon is a very cute piece. It has an unusual combination of fruits. The cherry head has a built-in drip-dry spoon with a hole that is attached underneath her lid. This piece stands 5-1/2 inches high and is not signed. Value: $35-$45.

Unsigned chefs oil & vinegar—$105-$115 for set; egg cups—$15-$20 each (from Dworkin Collection; photo by Van Blerck Photography).

CHEFS OIL & VINEGAR AND EGG CUPS (UNSIGNED)

This chef set is not signed, but has a blue and white rectangular paper sticker label which reads "Japan." All of the pieces to the set are ceramic. The oil & vinegar stands 7-1/4 inches high; the mustard pot is 4-1/4 inches high. The pieces store neatly in their red-and-white striped metal canopy organizer. The identical oil & vinegar has turned up in plastic composition, also. The matching egg cups are 3-3/4 inches tall. There are many other kitchen-related items that match this set. Value: cruet set—$105-$115; egg cups—$15-$20 each.

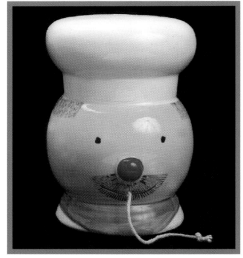

Unsigned chefs string holder: $50-$60 (from Dworkin Collection; photo by Van Blerck Photography).

CHEF STRING HOLDER

This Chef string holder is part of the cruet set pictured in this section. He measures 5-1/2 inches high and is not signed, but has a blue rectangular paper sticker that reads "Japan." Value: $50-$60.

Unsigned dog string holder: $45-$55 (from Dworkin Collection; photo by Van Blerck Photography).

Dog String Holder (unsigned)

This Dog string holder is a Holt-Howard look-a-like. The cute dog has the same face, expressive eyes and whiskers as Holt-Howard's famous cat string holder, and its scarf and scissors holder mimic the cat's. This pooch is 4-1/4 inches high by 4-3/4 inches wide. Most people think that he's related to the cat, but he's not Holt-Howard. This string-pull has a blue rectangular paper sticker that reads "Japan." Value: $45-$55.

Unsigned pixie rye decanter, with mustache: $75-$85 (from Dworkin Collection; photo by Van Blerck Photography).

Unsigned pixie rye decanter, with no mustache: $75-$85 (from Dworkin Collection; photo by Van Blerck Photography).

Pixie Decanters—"How Dry I Am" (unsigned)

Many collectors associate these decanters with Holt-Howard's Pixieware line because of their pixie-type faces and the style of lettering on top of their heads. Each decanter is 11-1/2 inches tall and has a built-in music box beneath its base. When the decanter is lifted, the music box plays "How Dry I Am." Although both of these pixies read "Rye" on top of their heads, they are different. There is also a scotch decanter and surely more pieces to this set. These pieces are not signed and remain a mystery as to just which company was their manufacturer. Value: $75-$85 each.

Unsigned bourbon decanter: $35-$45 (from Dworkin Collection; photo by Van Blerck Photography).

BOURBON (UNSIGNED)

This bourbon's face bears a strong resemblance to the face on the Davar rye bottle. Both this bourbon and the Davar rye decanters have similar yellow vests and both of them hold a baton in their left hand. This bourbon fellow is very unusual in the sense that he comes equipped with four ceramic hooks that protrude from his base to accommodate four black shot glasses. This piece is not signed. Value: $35-$45.

Unsigned salt & pepper cats: $25-$35 for set (from collection of and photo by Janet Paruolo).

CATS SALT & PEPPER (UNSIGNED)

Although these salt & peppers are dead ringers for the Holt-Howard cats, they are not signed, and there isn't any historical Holt-Howard records on these shakers. This cheerful couple both have the famous Holt-Howard cat ears, and he wears the famous cat plaid; however, they are believed only to be a very good copies. Value: $35-$45 for the set

Unsigned cat yarn/string holder: $55-$65 (from Blair/Rodriguez Collection; photo by Mary Norman).

CAT YARN/STRING HOLDER (UNSIGNED)

Many collectors have this piece, and it is always showing up unsigned. To date, there's no proof that this cat yarn string holder is Holt-Howard, and there isn't any historical Holt-Howard records to confirm this piece as a Holt-Howard original. Value: $55-$65.

Cat plunger ashtray: $30-$35 (from collection of and photo by Darline Comisky).

CAT PLUNGER ASHTRAY (UNSIGNED)

Here's another "Cozy Kitten" Holt-Howard look alike. The top of the cat's head is an ashtray and has a push down plunger handle to dispose of ashes and store them in the cat's head. Value: $30-$35.

Viking mouse cheese crock: $25-$35 (from Dworkin Collection; photo by Van Blerck Photography).

MOUSE CHEESE CROCK

Many collectors confuse this cheese crock with Holt-Howard's Merry Mouse collection. This piece is 4-1/2 inches high and its lid is 4-1/2 inches in diameter. It says, "Our Favorite Stinky Cheese." It was made by Viking and is marked "Made in Japan." Value: $25-$35.

Unsigned gray mouse pencil sharpener: $20-$25 (from Blair/Rodriguez Collection; photo by Mary Norman).

GRAY MOUSE PENCIL SHARPENER (UNSIGNED)

This mouse pencil sharpener looks like it's related to the Holt-Howard Merry Mouse Series, but all the mice in that series were tan colored. Value: $20-$25.

Unsigned kangaroo bank: $45-$55 (from Blair/Rodriguez Collection; photo by Mary Norman).

KANGAROO BANK (UNSIGNED)

This "mama kangaroo with babies" bank has many Holt-Howard features; however, there isn't any information to date as to which company created it. Value: $45-$55.

This chapter is dedicated to anthropomorphic smiley-faced fruit, veggies and flowers. All of these pieces were being manufactured in the 1950s and 1960s and many were being sold on the marketplace around the same time as Holt-Howard's Pixiewares. Of course, these cute characters were all made in Japan, just like the rest of all their whimsical cousins.

Most of the collectibles in this section were created by PY and Napco; it's not unusual to find two of the same item and description with either signature on them. We have already explored the Napco Company in Chapter Seven, but PY was a very exciting company and worthy of some background information. Most collectors associate the PY name as a Japanese company, but PY was actually an American distributing company during the 1950s and 1960s. PY bought and imported all of its merchandise from Japan, and sold it to businesses in the United States. Today, these novelty condiment jars, cruets, shakers and cookie jars have become very collectible, and everyone adores their extremely expressive cartoon faces. This type of wonderful style is reminiscent of yesteryear and will probably never be captured in any porcelain collectibles again.

If you're collecting PY salt & peppers or oil & vinegar pieces for the first time, always make sure that you are buying a pair and not two duplicates. One easy way to identify matching sets is that almost all of these whimsical fruits, veggies and flowers are generally staring at each other (most of the time, their eyes are set in very flirtatious expressions).

PY red apple jam and jelly: $65-$75 (from Dworkin Collection; photo by Van Blerck Photography).

PY RED APPLE JAM AND JELLY

This red-apple couple stares lovingly at each other. They have removable lids to store jam and jelly and have their original spoons. This attached side-by-side condiment is signed "PY" and is 4 inches high. Value: $65-$75.

PY lemon jam and jelly: $65-$75 (from Dworkin Collection; photo by Van Blerck Photography).

PY LEMON JAM AND JELLY JARS

This lemon couple has removable lids with openings to accommodate spoons. One of these lemons is showing teeth in his smile! This attached side-by-side condiment is signed "PY" and is 4 inches high. Value: $65-$75.

PY cabbages with flower faces: jam jars—$65-$75; salt & pepper—$55-$65 for set (from Dworkin Collection; photo by Van Blerck Photography).

PY CABBAGES WITH FLOWER FACES SET

This is an unusual attached side-by-side cabbage jam and jelly condiment with flower faces and rose bud-handled lids. It has a matching salt & pepper with rose buds on their heads. All pieces are signed "PY" and both the side-by-side and shakers are 4 inches tall. Value: jars—$65-$75 for the set; salt & pepper—$55-$65 for set.

PY red apple oil & vinegar: $110-$120 for set (from Dworkin Collection; photo by Van Blerck Photography).

PY RED APPLE OIL & VINEGAR

The cruets in this red apple oil & vinegar set have an "O" or "V" to identify their contents. Both pieces have ceramic stoppers, are 7-1/2 inches tall and are signed "PY." Value: $110-$120 for the set.

PY pears and lemons oil & vinegar sets: $120 each (from Dworkin Collection; photo by Van Blerck Photography).

PEARS AND LEMONS OIL & VINEGAR SETS

These side-by-side pears and lemons form oil & vinegar cruets that are also joined at their heads. The ends of their pouring spouts identifies "O" for oil and "V" for vinegar. Both sets have cork stoppers and are 5-1/2 inches tall. Each set is signed "PY" and both also have a paper label that reads "Coronet." Value: $110-$120 each.

Onion oil & vinegar sets: No. 8301—$55-$65; GNCO—$55-$65 for set (from Dworkin Collection; photo by Van Blerck Photography).

ONION OIL & VINEGAR SETS

This single onion oil & vinegar branches out into two pouring spouts—one for oil and one for vinegar. The letters "O" and "V" designate each compartment. This piece is not signed, but has identification No. 8301 (could be Napco). Value: No. 8301—$55-$65.

The oil companion to this other set appears very concerned as she watches her mate crying his eyes out. The pair stand 5-1/2 inches and both have a paper sticker that reads "GNCO." Value: GNCO—$55-$65 for the set.

PY lemon tea pot—$135-$155; PY lemon sugar & creamer—$55-$65 for set (photo Van Blerck Photography).

PY Lemon Tea Pot and Creamer & Sugar

This lemon tea pot measures 6 inches high and is size signed "PY." The lemon covered-sugar (4-1/4 inches) and creamer (3-3/4 inches), also signed "PY," are part of the same set that includes pieces such as a cookie jar, planter and wall pocket. One interesting characteristic about the lemon is that, with the exception of the side-by-side jam jars, all of these lemons stare to their left—even the creamer and sugar do not stare at each other! Value: tea pot—$135-$155; sugar & creamer—$55-$65 for the set.

PY red apple tea pot—$135-$155; Miyao red apple sugar & creamer—$55-$65 for set: (photo Van Blerck Photography).

Red Apple Tea Pot and Sugar & Creamer

The red apple tea pot 6 inches tall is signed "PY"; however, the matching sugar (4-1/2 inches) & creamer (3-1/2 inches) are signed "Miyao." Value: tea pot—$135-$155; sugar & creamer—$55-$65 for the set.

PY yellow apple cup and saucer—$35-$45 for set; tea pot—$135-$155(from Dworkin Collection; photo by Van Blerck Photography).

PY Yellow Apple Set

The yellow apple tea pot is 6 inches, the cup is 3 inches and the saucer is 6 inches in diameter. All are signed "PY." Value: tea pot—$135-$155; cup and saucer—$35-$45 for the set.

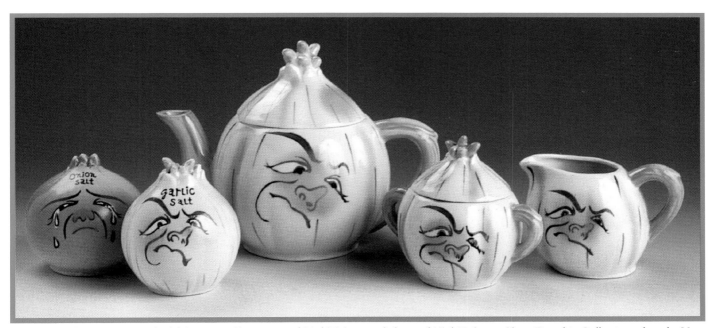

Unsigned garlic set: tea pot—$45-$50; sugar & creamer—$30-$35 for set; shakers—$15-$20 for set (from Dworkin Collection; photo by Van Blerck Photography).

Unsigned Garlic Set

Here's some real conversation pieces! A garlic tea pot (6 inches), creamer (3 inches) & sugar (4 inches) and garlic salt and onion salt shakers (3-1/2 inches). None of these annoyed characters are signed. Value: tea pot—$45-$50; sugar & creamer—$30-$35 for the set; shakers—$15-$20 for the set.

PY yellow and green apple string holders: $90-$100 each (from Dworkin Collection; photo by Van Blerck Photography).

PY APPLE STRING HOLDERS

These two string holders are not a pair, but certainly complement each other. Each apple can store a ball of string inside its head and both have an opening in their mouth to access and pull the needed amount of string.

These string holders were designed with a mounting hole in back so that they can be hung up on a wall. Both apples are 5 inches high and are signed "PY." Value: $90-$100 each.

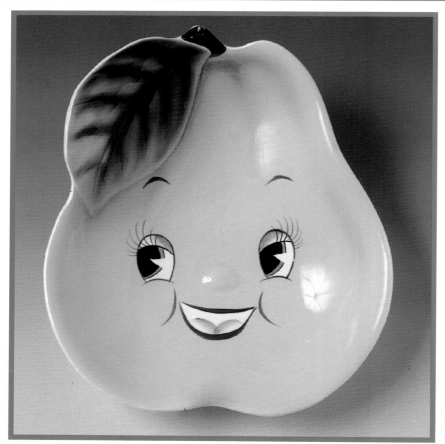

PEAR CHIP DISH

This yellow pear large chip dish is 10 inches by 8-3/4 inches, and is extra large to hold servings of potato chips or other snacks. Value: $50-$60.

Pear chip dish: $50-$60 (from Dworkin Collection; photo by Van Blerck Photography).

Miyao and PY pear cookie jars: $175-$200 each (from Dworkin Collection; photo by Van Blerck Photography).

MIYAO AND PEAR COOKIE JARS

The yellow jar looks happy, but the green jar is unhappy and crying (it's an oddity). The jars have a green leaf and pink bow (with polka dots) as handles. Both jars are 7 inches high. The crying jar is signed "Miyao" pottery; the smiling jar is signed "PY." Value: $175-$200 each.

Miyao red apple and PY lemon cookie jars: $190-$200 each (from Dworkin Collection; photo by Van Blerck Photography).

APPLE AND LEMON COOKIE JARS

This red apple cookie jar is typical of the other pieces to this set that are always wide-eyed and smiling. She has two green leaves as her handles, is 6-1/2 inches high and signed "Miyao." The lemon cookie jar wears a large bonnet of green which serves as her lid. She is 6-1/2 inches high and signed "PY." Value: $190-$200 each.

Cookie jars: Grantcrest red apple—$150-$175; unsigned lemon—$125-$150 (from Dworkin Collection; photo by Van Blerck Photography).

APPLE AND LEMON COOKIE JARS

The adorable red apple cookie has large flirtatious blue eye lids and is signed "Grantcrest." This apple has brown handles and is 7 inches high. The bizarrely multicolored cookie jar is most likely a lemon, since much of its surface has a pitted texture. This piece has nice yellow handles, is 7 inches high and not signed. Value: Grantcrest red apple—$150-$175; unsigned lemon—$125-$150.

Watermelon planter—$65-$75; salt & pepper—$55-$65 for set (from collection of and photo by Francine Sholty).

WATERMELON PLANTER AND SHAKERS

Mama watermelon planter sports a proud smile while watching over her offspring salt & pepper shakers. Value: planter—$65-$75; salt & pepper—$55-$65 for the set.

PY pear and "N" strawberry planters: $45-$55 each (from Dworkin Collection; photo by Van Blerck Photography).

STRAWBERRY AND PEAR PLANTERS

The strawberry planter 4-1/2 inches high and signed with letter "N" in circle. The PY yellow pear planter is a perfect match to the pear cookie jar in this section; it has the same pink eyelids and pink bow on her head and is 4-1/2 inches high. Value: $45-$55 each.

Planters—Miyao lemon and PY red apple: $45-$55 each (from Dworkin Collection; photo by Van Blerck Photography).

LEMON AND RED APPLE PLANTERS

The lemon planter is 4-1/2 inches signed "Miyao." The red apple planter 5 inches tall and signed "PY." Value: $45-$55 each.

Planters (unidentified maker): $45-$50 each (from Dworkin Collection; photo by Van Blerck Photography).

VARIOUS PLANTERS

All three of these planters were made by the same unknown company, since they all are stamped with the same small olive branch peace wreath and read, "Hand Painted Japan." The corn on cob with a hat is 5 inches, the cabbage is 4 inches, and the black-faced sunflower wall pocket is 5 inches. Value: $45-$50 each.

PY lemon wall pocket: $65-$75 (from Dworkin Collection; photo by Van Blerck Photography).

LEMON WALL POCKET

Although this lemon is shaped like a tea pot, it is actually a wall pocket. There is a mounting hole in the back for a nail to hang it on the wall. It is 5 inches and signed "PY." Value: $65-$75.

PY Sunflower Wall Pocket

This smiling sunflower is a wall pocket. It is 6-1/2 inches high and signed "PY." Value: $65-$75.

PY sunflower wall pocket: $65-$75 (from Dworkin Collection; photo by Van Blerck Photography).

"Made in Japan" mama sunflower and babies: $85-$95 for set (from Dworkin Collection; photo by Van Blerck Photography).

MAMA SUNFLOWER AND TWO BABIES

This mama sunflower is 7-1/2 inches. She isn't complete unless she is accompanied with her two baby sunflowers (4- 3/4 inches). All three pieces to this set are wall pockets and stamped "Made in Japan." Value: $85-$95 for the set.

PY pears and apples salt & peppers: $40-$50 for each set (from Dworkin Collection; photo by Van Blerck Photography).

PY PEARS AND APPLES SALT & PEPPERS

The yellow apple salt & pepper are 3 inches high and the yellow pears are 4 inches. Both sets are signed "PY." Value: $40-$50 for each set.

PY strawberries and pineapples girls salt & peppers: $55-$65 for each set (from Dworkin Collection; photo by Van Blerck Photography).

PY STRAWBERRIES AND PINEAPPLES SALT & PEPPERS

The pineapple girls and strawberry girls salt & peppers are both are signed "PY." Value: $55-$65 for each set.

Napco pears and lemons salt & peppers: $40-$50 for each set (from Dworkin Collection; photo by Van Blerck Photography).

NAPCO PEARS AND LEMONS SALT & PEPPERS

Both salt & pepper sets—pink and green pears with hats and lemons with pink faces—have the Napco foil sticker. Value: $40-$50 for each set.

Salt & peppers: PY lemons—$45-$55 for set; Napco pears—$40-$50 for set (from Dworkin Collection; photo by Van Blerck Photography).

LEMONS AND PEARS SALT & PEPPERS

The yellow lemons salt & pepper set with hats is signed "PY." The set of pink and green pears by Napco is a real whimsical novelty, since the salt shaker has an expression of being all shook up! Value: lemon—$45-$55 for set; pears—$40-$50 for set.

Napco salt & peppers with hats: $30-$40 for each set (from Dworkin Collection; photo by Van Blerck Photography).

NAPCO SALT & PEPPERS

The Napco-made salt & pepper sets (red apples with green and yellow caps and with white derby hats) are cute as a button. Value: $30-$40 for each set.

Napco pear set: $50-$60 for set (from Dworkin Collection; photo by Van Blerck Photography).

NAPCO PEAR SET

This cute set of miniature pears salt & peppers with matching mustard pot and leaf serving tray were made by Napco. Value: $50-$60 for the set.

PY flower-face salt & peppers: $35-$45 for each set (roses on left from Lori Smith Collection; others from Dworkin Collection; photo by Van Blerck Photography).

PY Flower Salt & Peppers

These three sets of adorable flower-face salt and peppers are signed "PY." Value: $35-$45 for each set.

PY sunflower salt & peppers: $25-$35 for set (from Dworkin Collection; photo by Van Blerck Photography).

Unsigned Sunflower Salt & Peppers

These unsigned sunflower heads stare at each other lovingly. They are not signed, but are stamped, "Japan."

Value: $25-$35 for the set.

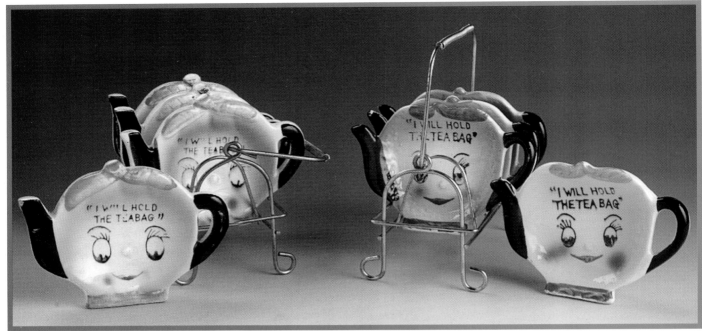

Davar and "Japan" tea bag-holder sets: $15-$20 each set (from Dworkin Collection; photo by Van Blerck Photography).

TEA BAG HOLDERS

Different companies made these tea bag holder sets. Each holder reads "I will hold the tea bag." Generally, these holders came in a set of four with a stacking metal brass stand to accommodate them. All these smiling faces are fruit heads, shaped like tea pots. Each tea bag holder is capable of standing on its own. The set on the right is signed "Japan" and the set on the left is "Davar." Value: $15-$20 per set.

Tea bag holders: $3-$4 each (from Dworkin Collection; photo by Van Blerck Photography).

TEA BAG HOLDERS

This red apple tea bag holder stands on its own, and sports a cute derby hat similar to many of the salt & pepper sets in this chapter (this piece is No. B2678). The yellow pear is signed "PY" and cannot stand on its own. Value: $3-$4 each.

Holt-Howard hit a home run when it created these adorable kittens for the kitchen. Everyone loves these irresistible cartoon-like kitties, not to mention the fact that these whimsical characters became the perfect gift to buy for millions of cat lovers all over the country during their debut in the late 1950s.

Today, these cute tabbies and toms are one of the hottest cat collectibles in the country and are giving fellow cousins like Garfield, Felix, Kliban Cat and Tom & Jerry a real run for the money. Although Holt-Howard called these "Cozy Kitchen Kitties," many of the pieces were versatile enough to be used in other rooms of the house. After the success of these cats, other companies began to copy the Holt-Howard style, but they have never really been able to capture the personalities and expressiveness of these felines.

These kittens were made around the same time as the Pixiewares, starting in 1958 and continuing into the early 1960s. Unfortunately, some of the cats were not signed and only had a foil sticker which often fell off. Most of the kittens in this series have either polka-dotted or plaid scarves around their necks; however, this is not always the case, since the sugar and soap shakers, merry measure and butter dish do not wear scarves. The male kittens wear scarves of blue or green with polka dots, while the females wear pink scarves with polka dots. Some other cats wear dark pink and black plaid scarves. Many of the cat pieces have the famous green and black plaid incorporated into their design. Some male cats wear the plaid pattern design on their hats, while the plaid is also used on pillows and around other border designs through out the set.

Also in this chapter, we are going to visit just a few British "Cozy Kitchen Kitties" that were made in England, as part of Holt-Howard, but released by the John E. Beck & Co.

In today's collectible market place, some of Holt-Howard's cats are still common while others are as rare to find as "hen's teeth."

Note: In addition to the ceramic pieces in this "Cozy Kitchen Kitties" series, Holt-Howard also created a fabric toaster cover, wall cache and napkin holder.

Salt & peppers: $15-$20 for set (from collection of and photo by Darline Comisky).

Cozy Kittens Salt & Peppers

This salt & pepper set has almost become an icon of the Holt-Howard company because they are always in plentiful supply at flea markets and collectible shows. Everyone loves this set that stands 4-1/2 inches high and has noise mechanisms underneath that go "meow" when turned upside down. Due to their age, it's rare that you will find the "meow" mechanisms working. It is believed that over time the tiny reeds inside the voice mechanisms expand with moisture and need to be reshaped in order to work again. Be thrilled if you find one that still works! This set is copyrighted 1958. Value: $15-$20 for the set.

Peeking pets in basket salt & peppers: $30-$35 for set (from collection of and photo by Darline Comisky).

Peeking Pets in Basket Salt & Peppers

These salt & pepper peeking pets were sold in their own wicker baskets and stand 3 inches high. Why the

Peeking pets outside their baskets. (from collection of and photo by Darline Comisky).

baskets? Holt-Howard said "no particular reason, just cute, we guess." Value: $30-$35 for the set.

Winky-blinky "meow" salt & peppers: $35-$40 for set (from Blair/Rodriguez Collection; photo by Mary Norman).

WINKY-BLINKY "MEOW" SALT & PEPPERS

This winky blinky salt & pepper set wink, blink and meow when lifted. Their tails serve as handles to make pouring easy. The pair stand 4-1/2 inches high. Value: $35-$40 for the set.

String holders: $40-$50 each (from Dworkin Collection; photo by Van Blerck Photography).

KITTEN STRING HOLDERS

These strings holders are made to hang on the wall and came equipped with a opening in their scarves to accommodate a pair of scissors. The proud cat with center focused eyes measures 4-1/2 inches wide by 4-1/2 inches high and is copyrighted 1958. The second cat was quite a find with eyes looking to its right and eye lashes. The right looking cat is larger and measures 5

inches wide by 4-3/4 inches high and appears to be copyrighted 1959. Both pieces were originally sold with scissors in the box. Value: $40-$50 each.

Memo minder: $75-$80 (from Blair/Rodriguez Collection; photo by Mary Norman).

KITTEN MEMO MINDER

This kitten "Memo Minder" hangs on the wall equipped with a pad and pencil; it is 6 inches high. This piece was originally sold with an enclosed "1960 year calendar," so it was versatile enough to be used either as a memo minder or calendar. Value: $75-$80.

Merry measure: $70-$80 (from Blair/Rodriguez Collection; photo by Mary Norman).

COZY KITTEN MERRY MEASURE

The Cozy Kittens "Merry Measure" is a great sewing room collectible and is 3 inches by 3-1/2 inches. The kitten's red felt tongue pulls out and becomes a 36-inch tape measure, while the pillow's lid is removable for storing pins, needles, clips or whatever you have. This piece is copyrighted 1958. Value: $70-$80.

Cottage cheese crock: $45-$55 (from Blair/Rodriguez Collection; photo by Mary Norman).

COZY KITTENS COTTAGE CHEESE CROCK

The Cozy Kittens "Cottage Cheese" crock is 4-1/2 inches by 4-1/2 inches. The container's lid is removable and holds 8 ounces of cottage cheese. This piece is copyrighted 1958. Value: $45-$55.

Caddy—$55-$60; napkin holder/salt & peppers—$45-$55 (from Blair/Rodriguez Collection; photo by Mary Norman).

COZY KITTENS CADDY & NAPKIN HOLDER/ SALT & PEPPERS

This Cozy Kittens caddy is 6-1/2 inches high and has an open pocket atop its head for the storage of pens and pencils. The spring on the kitten's back holds letters. Copyrighted 1958, this piece is also very versatile since it can be used at the table and can hold flowers and napkins. The Cozy Kittens seasoners/napkin rack is 7-1/2 by 3 inches. The salt and pepper shakers sit nicely at each end of the highly polished brass rack, which can hold up to 20 napkins. Value: caddy—$55-$60; napkin holder/salt & peppers—$45-$55.

Bud vases: $80-$90 for pair (from Blair/Rodriguez Collection; photo by Mary Norman).

COZY KITTENS BUD VASES

Holt-Howard called this pair "Tabby and Tom Charmers." This two-piece set of Cozy Kittens flower bud vases are 6-3/4 inches high and both have openings on top of their heads to accommodate cut flowers. The boy kitten wears the traditional Holt-Howard green and black plaid design in his hat. This set is copyrighted 1958. Value: $80-$90 for the pair.

Ashtray/match holder: $55-$65 (from Blair/Rodriguez Collection; photo by Mary Norman).

COZY KITTEN ASHTRAY/MATCH HOLDER

This kitten sits on the traditional plaid pillow which is an ashtray that measures 4-1/2 inches across. The kitten extends his paw upwards to his cheek to hold a shiny brass matchbook holder. This piece is copyrighted 1958. Value: $55-$65.

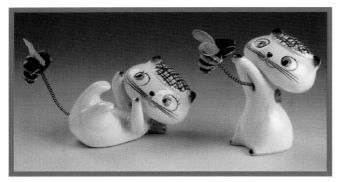

Bee bothered: $45-$55 for set (from Dworkin Collection; photo by Van Blerck Photography).

COZY KITTENS "BEE BOTHERED" KITTENS

This whimsical pair of "Bee Bothered" Cozy Kittens are 3 inches long and have fabric bees attached to their bodies by a spring. When the kittens are moved, the bees dance all around and create a truly fun decoration for a flower pot, table arrangement or shelf. These kittens wear the famous plaid decoration as hats and were sold as a set. Value: $45-$55 for the set.

Wall caddy: $70-$80 (from Blair/Rodriguez Collection; photo by Mary Norman).

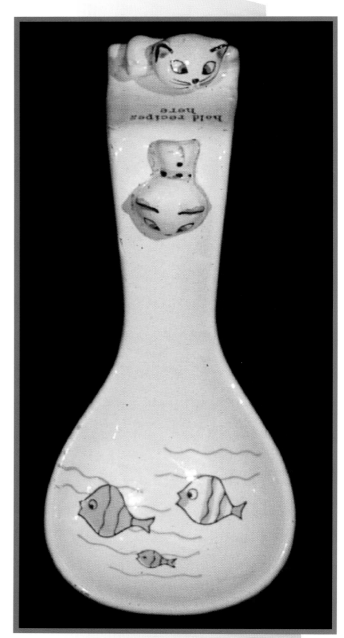

Spoon rest: $65-$75 (from Blair/Rodriguez Collection; photo by Mary Norman).

COZY KITTEN WALL CADDY

This wall caddy is very versatile and can hold keys, wrist watches, trinkets and many other items on its tail or arm. The kitten's head has an opening on top to either serve as a planter or to accommodate cut flowers. This wall caddy was originally sold as a two-piece set since it came equipped with a circular metal key ring hanger that hung from the kitten's tail. This piece is about 7 inches long from the curve of his tail to the tip of his ear; however, the entire piece (with ring) would measure 11 inches, complete with key ring. Value: $70-$80.

COZY KITTENS SPOON REST

Holt-Howard advertised this decorative spoon rest as a "Stove topper delight" since it serves as a spoon rest and holds recipes. It is 6 inches long. Value: $65-$75.

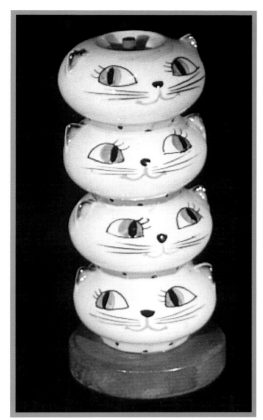

Stacking seasons: $50-$60 for set (from Blair/Rodriguez Collection; photo by Mary Norman).

COZY KITTENS STACKING SEASONS

This totem-pole style of stacking seasons stands 5 inches high and is comprised of two salts and two peppers. The set is very portable and stacks neatly on its wooden rack. Each kitten wears a different colored bow around its neck. Value: $50-$60 for the set.

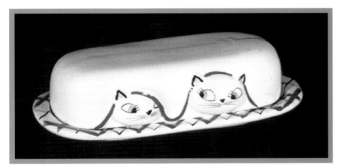

Butter dish: $95-$105 (from Blair/Rodriguez Collection; photo by Mary Norman).

COZY KITTENS BUTTER DISH

Two adorable young kittens peak out from beneath a tablecloth design which is the lid to this 7-inch butter dish. On the back side of the tablecloth, the kittens' tails stick out and are lovingly locked together. The underplate's border is decorated in the famous cat plaid. This two-piece set is perfect for holding a quarter-pound stick of butter and is copyrighted 1958. Value: $95-$105.

Sugar & creamer: $55-$65 for set (from Blair/Rodriguez Collection; photo by Mary Norman).

COZY KITTEN SUGAR & CREAMER

This three-piece set is stackable and comprised of the creamer on bottom and covered sugar on top. The kitten wears the traditional plaid hat that is the lid to the sugar bowl. This piece stands 4-1/4 inches and is copyrighted 1959. Value: $55-$65 for the set.

Sugar shaker: $55-$65 (from Blair/Rodriguez Collection; photo by Mary Norman).

COZY KITTEN SUGAR SHAKER

This pretty little miss is a sugar shaker and stands 6-1/4 inches high. This piece performs two functions since she is capable of either shaking sugar from either atop her head, or pouring it out from her sugar pour sack on the side. A tight-fitting cork plug seals the pouring spout when not in use. Value: $55-$65.

Soap shaker: $60-$70 (from Blair/Rodriguez Collection; photo by Mary Norman).

COZY KITTEN SOAP SHAKER

This busy house cleaner is a soap shaker and capable of holding 12 ounces of detergent or cleanser. She stands 6-3/4 inches tall. There are seven holes atop her head to shake out the contents and a large cork plug in the base. Value: $60-$70.

Match Dandy: $65-$75 (from Blair/Rodriguez Collection; photo by Mary Norman).

COZY KITTENS MATCH DANDY

This cat is all grown up and smoking a pipe! He holds matches in the opening atop of his head. His coat is stippled for scratching to strike matches, and another opening in the cat's back accommodates used matches. This dapper cat is "dressed to the nines" while sporting the famous plaid cat cap, a handsome coordinated sport jacket and a cane on his arm. Value: $65-$75.

Kitty catch clip: $25-$35 (from Blair/Rodriguez Collection; photo by Mary Norman).

COZY KITTEN KITTY CATCH CLIP

The clip portion of this "Kitty Catch" clip is chrome-plated and the entire piece measures 4-3/4 inches. Holt-Howard referred to this piece as a "Sure Action Clip." It is multi-functional and can be used for towels, paper bags, lunch containers, bibs or just notes. Value: $25-$35.

Spice set: $100-$110 for set (from Blair/Rodriguez Collection; photo by Mary Norman).

COZY KITTENS SPICE SET

Mama cat and three baby kittens comprise this adorable spice set. The four pieces hang from a vertical black wrought-iron wall rack, with mama cat on top, then nutmeg, paprika and cinnamon kittens descending below her. The entire five-piece set (when displayed complete with rack) measures 10 inches. Value: $100-$110 for the complete five-piece set.

Condiment jars—ketchup, mustard and jam 'n jelly: $150-$165 each (from Dworkin Collection; photo by Van Blerck Photography).

COZY KITTENS CONDIMENT JARS

The kitten condiment jars (Ketchup, Mustard and Jam 'n Jelly) are part of a series of five jars and a cream crock that were featured in a 1962 Holt-Howard catalog. Interestingly enough, the mustard and ketchup have attached spreaders (just like the Pixiewares), instead of scoop style spoons that the Jam 'n Jelly has. John Howard informed me that these adorable condiments were not manufactured on as large a scale as some of the earlier cat series and consequently are a harder find in today's collectible marketplace. Value: $150-$165 each.

Instant coffee: $150-$165 (from Ann and Ken Storms Collection, photo by Chris Camera Center).

COZY KITTEN INSTANT COFFEE

A fourth jar to the cat condiment series is "Instant Coffee," which has blue splotches on its base and a blue halo surrounding the kitten's face. It also has the seal-tight white ring around its lid and a scoop spoon attached, just like the Pixieware Instant Coffee. All of these jars have spoons attached to the kittens' lids and each is 5 inches tall. This condiment series is not signed, but was featured in Holt-Howard's catalogs. Value: $150-$165.

COZY KITTEN SUGAR & CREAMER

The fifth condiment jar to this set is a "Lil' Sugar" (5 inches), with a cat's head on top of the lid, and a matching "Cream Crock" (2-1/4 inches). The Lil' Sugar cat has the same pink coloration as the Jam 'n Jelly cat condiment (pictured at left). Value: $165-$185 for the set.

"Meow" oil & vinegar: $175+ for set (from Blair/Rodriguez Collection; photo by Mary Norman).

COZY KITTENS "MEOW" OIL & VINEGAR

These kitten cruets stare lovingly at each other in true Holt-Howard fashion and are 8 inches tall. The oil & vinegar both "meow" when lifted to perform their tasks. The boy wears the famous plaid hat and has an "V" for vinegar inscribed on his front, while his companion piece has the "O" for oil. These loving kittens were sold as a pair. Value: $175+ for set.

"Meow" mug with squeaker: $25-$35 (from Blair/Rodriguez Collection; photo by Mary Norman).

COZY KITTEN "MEOW" MUG WITH SQUEAKER

This 8-ounce mug has a lift-and-listen squeaker. Value: $25-$35.

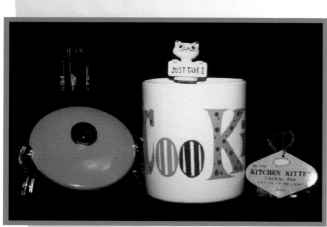

Cookie jar: $250+ (from collection of and photo by Darline Comisky).

COZY KITTEN POP-UP COOKIE JAR

This cookie jar stands 6-1/4 inches high. Every time the lid is lifted, a kitty pops up and display's a sign that reads "Just Take One." Value: $250+

"Meow" pitcher: $95-$105 (from collection of and photo by Darline Comisky).

COZY KITTEN "MEOW" PITCHER

This pouring pitcher is 7-1/2 inches tall, and holds 24 ounces of liquids. The bottom of the pitcher has a "lift' n listen" squeaker and is copyrighted 1960. The pitcher was sold separately from the adorable four ounces "lift' n listen" cups that match it. Value: $95-$105.

"Meow" cups: $35 each (this photo is from a Holt-Howard catalog).

COZY KITTENS "MEOW" CUPS

These 4-ounce "lift' n listen" kitty cups match the 24 ounce cat pouring pitcher. The cups were sold as a pair, two to the box. Value: $35 each.

Grease crock: $95-$105 (this photo is from a Holt-Howard catalog).

Cozy Kitten Grease Crock

The "Keeper of the Grease" crock is 4" in diameter and is especially useful for the storage of bacon and other fats. Value: $95-$105.

Cheese board: $85-$95 (from John E. Beck & Co., catalog; photo by Van Blerck Photography).

Cozy Kittens Cheese Board (England)

There's a strong possibility that this cat cheese board was either manufactured in England or Portugal by John E. Beck & Co., and appeared in its 1961 Christmas catalog. Even though this piece is Holt-Howard, it should be signed "J.B." for John E. Beck & Co. Value: $85-$95.

Butter dish: $120-$125 (from John E. Beck & Co., catalog; photo by Van Blerck Photography).

Cozy Kittens Butter Dish (England)

This covered butter is very different and was strictly made for the British marketplace. The two kittens on the top lid are reminiscent of the 1958 Cozy Kittens Cottage Cheese Crock, but this base is quite different. This butter dish was displayed in a 1961 Christmas catalog of John E. Beck & Co. ltd., London, England. Value: $120-$125.

Coin kitty: $95-$100 (from John E. Beck & Co., catalog; photo by Van Blerck Photography).

Cozy Kitten Coin Kitty (England)

This is a British Coin Kitty as he appeared in the John E. Beck 1962 and 1963 Christmas catalogs. This proud cat bank wears the famous plaid cap and bears the English monetary pound sign on his scarf. There was also a girl "sixpenny kitty" bank. Her eyes stared to her left and she wore a polka-dot scarf. Value: $95-$100 each.

Salt & peppers: $75-$85 for set (from John E. Beck & Co., catalog; photo by Van Blerck Photography).

Sugar & creamer: $85-$95 for set (this photo is from a Holt-Howard catalog).

COZY KITTENS SALT & PEPPERS (ENGLAND)

Although this salt & pepper duo look familiar, they are the British version. In England, the male cat wears the famous plaid cap! This pair also appeared in the John E. Beck 1962 and 1963 Christmas catalogs. Value: $75-$85 for the set.

COZY KITTENS SUGAR & CREAMER

This three-piece set is comprised of a covered sugar bowl which is 5 inches tall, and a creamer that stands 4 inches tall. The creamer has a lift and listen "meow" squeaker. Value: $85-$95 for the set.

Cozy Kittens original boxes (from the John Clay and Judy Shute Collection; photo by Van Blerck Photography).

COZY KITTENS ORIGINAL BOXES

These are two original Cozy Kitten boxes: twine holder and salt & pepper set. The twine holder has a rectangular red and white inspection label with numbers; it reads "Passed" and "Made In Japan."

Roosters have always been and continue to be a highly collectible item. Holt-Howard incorporated the collectibility of roosters with a beautifully stylish colored tabletop accessory group set which the company named "COQ ROUGE" (French for red rooster). And, as Holt-Howard stated in its advertising, this crisp and striking set is certainly worth crowing about!

John Howard told me that during the late 1950s, Holt-Howard believed that the kitchen's role in the average American household was drastically changing. The kitchen was becoming a place for families to come together for a meal or socialize while the meal was being prepared, rather than just a small room to prepare food. With this marketing strategy in mind, Holt-Howard designed COQ ROUGE and advertised it as "Table Flair" to brighten up and decorate America's kitchens. And just for the record, this beautiful set was designed by Robert Howard.

The first pieces of this set were released in 1960; additional items were introduced to the pattern as it increased in popularity through 1964. During the mid 1960s through early 1970s, Holt-Howard maintained kitchen collection concepts displays in many major stores such as Sears, Macy's, J.C. Penny's, Bullocks and B. Altman's. These displays were called "Kitchen Fashions by Holt-Howard" and many were quite extensive, featuring coffee mugs, cookie jars, salt & peppers, trivets, spoon rests and canisters, along with coordinates such as COQ ROUGE. Holt-Howard also designed and manufactured other dinnerware patterns such as "Terraware," "Orchardware," "Apple Jack" and others, but COQ ROUGE appears to be the most sought after pattern today and evidently one of the company's most famous patterns. COQ ROUGE was a complete breakfast service set and offered accessories such as salt & peppers, napkin holders, egg cups, candle holders and butter dishes.

The wonderful part about this set is not only its gaily colored pattern and serviceability, but the giftware portion of the set contains numerous beautiful figural pieces that are highly sought-after in today's marketplace. The giftware items were so extensive that they even included ashtrays and a vase, plus color-matched felt, burlap and wooden accessories, including: 10-inch pot holder; 24-inch fly swatter; 13-inch by 24-inch kitchen wall caddy; 14-inch tote bag with vinyl interior; 14-inch memo minder; 40-inch yard stick caddy with pocket for scissors; 8-inch by 15-inch breadboard; nest of baskets ranging from 6 inches to 8 inches; 8-inch placemats; and an 8-inch twine holder and scissors.

Most of the ceramic items in this set were signed in black letters which read "Holt-Howard" and the copyright year, plus the black and gold "HH" paper sticker. The famous gaily colored rooster in shades of red, orange, yellow, brown, ochre and white appears on the majority of pieces, with the exception of the creamer and coffee saucers.

Dinner plate: $12-$15 (from Blair/Rodriguez Collection; photo by Mary Norman).

DINNER PLATE

This dinner plate measures 9-1/2 inches. Copyrighted 1962. Value: $12-$15.

Cereal bowl: $12-$15 (from collection of and photo by Darline Comisky).

CEREAL BOWL

This cereal bowl measures 6 inches in diameter. Copyrighted 1962. Value: $12-$15.

Sugar & creamer: $35-$45 for set (from collection of and photo by Darline Comisky).

SUGAR & CREAMER

The sugar is 4-1/2 inches high, while the creamer is 2-1/2 inches high. Copyrighted 1961. Value: $35-$45 for the set.

Pitcher, 32 oz.—$60; coffee mugs—$12 each; snack tray $15 (from Blair/Rodriguez Collection; photo by Mary Norman).

PITCHER, COFFEE MUGS AND SNACK TRAY

This juice pitcher is copyrighted 1964. Due to the success of this set, pitchers were made in at least three different sizes—12 oz., 32 oz. and 48 oz. The coffee mugs are 10-ounce size and were sold four to a box. The snack tray is indented to hold a coffee cup securely in place and was featured in Holt-Howard's catalog with a solid-gold coffee mug that was color-coordinated to match the gold colors in the rooster. Value: pitchers—12 oz., $45, 32 oz., $60, 48 oz., $75; mugs—$12 each; snack tray—$15.

Small salt & peppers: $8-12 for set (from Dworkin Collection; photo by Van Blerck Photography).

SMALL SALT & PEPPERS

There are two sets of shakers to this set. The one pictured here is the smaller version and only stands 3-3/4 inches high vs. the standard 4-1/2 inch set. The larger set has the "S" and "P" printed on the roosters' chests, but this smaller set does not. Value: $8-$12 for the small set.

Snack dish—$15; large salt & peppers—$20-$30 for set; napkin holder—$25-$35 (from Blair/Rodriguez Collection; photo by Mary Norman).

NUT DISH, SALT & PEPPERS & NAPKIN HOLDER

This rooster nut dish was sold as part of a table-tray set of four pieces, all identical in size and shape, measuring 4-3/4 inches each. The pieces were used for nuts, jam, condiments or even for individual ashtrays. The larger 4-1/2 inch salt & peppers are copyrighted 1960. The napkin holder is 7 inches high and has two holes at its top so it can also be used as a wall hanger; it is copyrighted 1961. Value: snack dish—$15; salt & peppers—$20-$30 for the set; napkin holder—$25-$35.

Coffee server—$50-$60; cookie jar—$95-$110 (from Blair/Rodriguez Collection; photo by Mary Norman).

COFFEE SERVER AND COOKIE JAR

The covered coffee server holds 36 ounces and is copyrighted 1960. The cookie jar is 7-3/4 inches by 5-3/4 inches and is copyrighted 1961. Value: coffee server—$50-$60; cookie jar—$95-$110.

Coffee pot—$60-$70; cups—$12 each; trivet—$35 (from Blair/Rodriguez Collection; photo by Mary Norman).

COFFEE POT, CUPS AND TRIVET

This 6-cup coffee pot was sold as a hot-pot with a 5-foot cord. The coffee cups are 8-ounce size and were sold as a set of four. The trivet with tile is 5 inches by 9-3/4 inches. A larger, diamond-shaped 10-1/2 inch version of this trivet exists. Value: coffee pot—$60-$70; cups—$12 each; trivet—$35.

Jam 'n jelly—$35-$40; jam jar—$35-$40; pitcher—$25; egg cups—$15 each (from Blair/Rodriguez Collection; photo by Mary Norman).

JAM 'N JELLY, JAM JAR, PITCHER & EGG CUPS

There are three condiments to this portion of the rooster set: ketchup, mustard and jam 'n jelly. All are similar in appearance and are 4 inches high. There's also an additional jam jar with the rooster perched on top that is 4-1/2 inches tall and is very similar in size and shape to the sugar jar. The small syrup pitcher pictured here is often mistaken as the creamer mate to the sugar bowl, but, as seen previously, the creamer is all white with only one red ring at its base. The egg cups measure 3-3/4 inches, are copyrighted 1961 and were sold as a four-piece set. There are two different sizes of egg cups to this set: one with a single red band on top and the other with a red band on its base. Value: jam 'n jelly—$30-$40; jam jar—$35-$40; syrup pitcher—$25; egg cups—$15 each.

Ketchup and mustard jars: $30-$40 each (from collection of and photo by Darline Comisky).

KETCHUP AND MUSTARD JARS

These two condiment jars match the jam 'n jelly jar (pictured at the top of this page) and are also 4 inches high. Copyrighted 1962. Value: $30-$40 each.

Candle holders—$25-$35 for pair; vase—$30-$35 (from Blair/Rodriguez Collection; photo by Mary Norman).

CANDLE HOLDERS AND VASE

The candle holders are 4-3/8 inches tall, were sold as a pair and are copyrighted 1960. The matching vase is 6 inches by 5 inches and copyrighted 1961. Value: candle holders—$25-$35 for the pair; vase—$30-$35.

Ashtrays—$15-$20 for pair; spoon rest—$20-$25 (from Blair/Rodriguez Collection; photo by Mary Norman).

ASHTRAYS AND SPOON REST

These 6-inch ashtrays are indented at rear of rooster to hold cigarettes and were sold as a pair. On top of the spoon rest, the rooster's head is indented on top to accommodate a spoon handle. The spoon rest is copyrighted 1961 and the ashtrays are 1964. Value: ashtrays—$15-$20 for the pair; spoon rest—$20-$25.

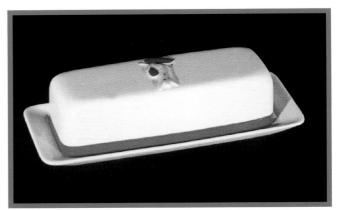

Butter dish: $40-$50 (from Blair/Rodriguez Collection; photo by Mary Norman).

BUTTER DISH

This butter dish is 6-3/4 inches long and shows off the gaily colored rooster on top of its lid. Copyrighted 1961. Value: $40-$50.

Wooden salt & peppers—$12-$15 for set; wooden recipe box—$65-$70 (from Blair/Rodriguez Collection; photo by Mary Norman).

WOODEN RECIPE BOX AND SALT & PEPPERS

This recipe box is made of wood and is 5-1/2 inches by 3-1/4 inches 4-1/4 inches. The wooden salt & pepper set is part of the wooden canister set; it measures 3-3/4 inches. Value: recipe box—$65-$70; salt & peppers—$12-$15 for the set.

Wooden canister set: $60-$65 for set of four (from Blair/Rodriguez Collection; photo by Mary Norman).

Wooden cigarette box: $35-$40 (from collection of and photo by Darline Comisky).

WOODEN CANISTER SET

This wooden flour canister is part of a four-unit set for storing flour, sugar, coffee and tea. The wooden salt and pepper set pictured on page 112 is part of this 10-piece set (including bottoms and lids). The pieces graduate in size from 3-3/4 inches (for the salt and peppers) up to 7 inches (for the flour canister). Value: $60-$65 for complete set of four canisters.

WOODEN CIGARETTE BOX

This wooden cigarette box is 11-3/4 inches long. It hangs on the wall and stores a full carton of cigarettes (there was also a companion wall-hanger match holder that is 11-3/4 inches long. All pieces feature the famous rooster. Value: $35-$40.

Holt-Howard created so many wonderful and unique figural collectibles that it would be almost impossible to describe all of them in one book. In this chapter, it is my intent to focus on mostly the whimsical side of Holt-Howard's collectibles, especially some of its more popular animal and figural novelty items that are so much in demand today at antiques and collectibles shows and flea markets. Here again, the time-frame that the majority of these collectibles were issued ranges from the late 1950s through the early 1960s. The items covered in this chapter encompass a wide variety of ceramics, including collectibles as small as candle rings and salt & peppers to others as large as banks.

Merry Mouse: cocktail kibitzers mice: $18-$23 each/$110-$120 for set of six (from Blair/Rodriguez Collection; photo by Mary Norman).

MERRY MOUSE: COCKTAIL KIBITZERS MICE

Holt-Howard called its mouse collection series "The Merry Mouse" and the company stated that "For every house we've got a mouse! Don't be nervous, they're made for service." All the mice in this series were created in the unique Holt-Howard "Ceramistripe" glaze. The Cocktail Kibitzers Mice were designed as cocktail accessories and they can hang on the side of a cocktail glass and have openings on the base of their backs to insert a toothpick. The toothpick would not only double as the mouse's tail, but was also used to hold cocktail cherries, olives, onions, etc. These adorable creatures stand 1-1/2 inches and were sold six per box with two dozen toothpicks. They appeared in the 1960 catalog. Value: $18- $23 each/$110-$120 for the complete set of six, in original, decorated gift box.

Merry Mouse: salt and peppers—$35-$40; desk mouse—$30-$35; cheese crock—$45-$55; match holder—$65-$75 (from Blair/Rodriguez Collection; photo by Mary Norman).

MERRY MOUSE: VARIOUS ITEMS

On the rear left of this photo is the Merry Mouse salt & pepper set. These shakers stand 3-3/4 inches tall and squeak when shaken. The pair stare lovingly at each other and both have three pouring holes in their heads. The male mouse has a small blue ribbon on his tail and the female has a red one. Since their bases have built-in squeakers, their refill spouts are located behind their heads. This pair is copyrighted 1958. Value: $35-$40.

In front of the salt & peppers is the Merry Mouse pencil sharpener that comes equipped with a sharpener behind his head. He is 3-1/4 inches and is part of a two-piece set called "Merry Mouse Desk Set." This set includes another mouse of the same height that has an opening in its head to hold pencils. These pieces appeared in the 1958 catalog. Value: $30-$35 each.

Also pictured here is the "Stinky Cheese Crock," which was specifically designed to make guests laugh at this unique container with a tight-fitting lid that seals in cheese odors. This piece is 4 inches in diameter and is copyrighted 1958. Value: $45-$55.

At the far right is the "Match Mouse," who has an opening in his head to hold wooden matches. The seat of his pants holds cigarettes and he has a rough textured "scratch on vest" to light matches. To be complete, the Match Mouse must have a cane in his right arm and a cigar in his mouth. This piece is not signed but was featured in the 1960 catalog. Value: $65-$75.

Merry Mouse: desk pen pal: $75-$85 (from Blair/Rodriguez Collection; photo by Mary Norman).

MERRY MOUSE: DESK PEN PAL

The Merry Mouse Desk Pen Pal is 5-1/2 inches by 5-1/2 inches and he sits on the lid to a storage box that stores stamps or paper clips. There is an opening in his lower back which holds a ball-point pen. This piece was sold individually; however, there is a Merry Mouse "Spindle Set" (6-1/4 inches by 4-1/2 inches) that's similar in appearance and has a very tall tail for holding elusive notes and receipts. Both mouse pieces were featured in the 1958 catalog. Value: $75-$85 each.

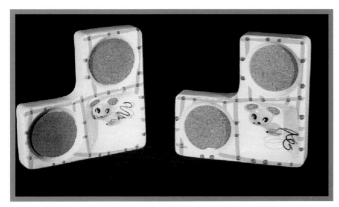

Merry Mouse: corner coaster/ashtray: $45-$55 each (from Blair/Rodriguez Collection; photo by Mary Norman).

MERRY MOUSE: CORNER COASTER/ASHTRAY

The Merry Mouse corner coaster/ashtray is comprised of two coasters (one in each corner).These coasters are set into a weighted ceramic holder for stick-free beverage service. The mouse portion of these pieces is an ashtray. The mice come equipped with coiled tails to hold cigarettes. These coasters appeared in the 1960 Holt-Howard catalog. Value: $45-$55 each.

Jeeves: cherries, olives and onions jars: $125+ each (from Blair/Rodriguez Collection; photo by Mary Norman).

JEEVES: CHERRIES, OLIVES AND ONIONS JARS

These fun and zesty fellows have been nicknamed "The Butler Series" by collectors and dealers all over the country; however, their actual name is "Jeeves." This "If You Please" bar set is done in bright red with white, black and gold and is a real eye-catcher and crowd-pleaser. The olive jar has a built-in metal spear to grab those elusive olives, while the cherries and onion jars have drip-dry spoons to drain liquids. All pieces stand 5 inches tall and are copyrighted 1960; olives is copyrighted 1961. The entire set was featured in Holt-Howard's 1961 catalog. Value: $125+ each.

Jeeves: decanter: $150+ (from Dworkin Collection; photo by Van Blerck Photography).

JEEVES: DECANTER

The "Jeeves" decanter holds a bisque sign for writing on "contents" and a cork stopper to keep your favorite libation fresh. The decanter stands 10-1/2 inches tall and is copyrighted 1960. Value: $150+.

Jeeves: martini shaker set— $180+ for set (from Blair/Rodriguez Collection; photo by Mary Norman).

JEEVES: MARTINI SHAKER SET

The Jeeves martini set is comprised of a shaker and four, 4-ounce tumblers. The shaker holds 18 ounces of martini mix and his head has a muddler attached for stirring. Value: $180+ for the set.

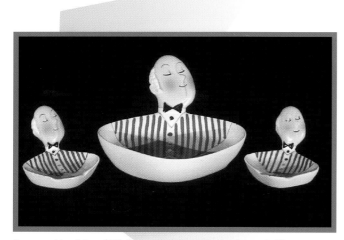

Jeeves: chip dish—$75-$80; ashtrays—$45-$55 each (from Blair/Rodriguez Collection; photo by Mary Norman).

JEEVES: CHIP DISH AND ASHTRAYS

This chip dish is 6-3/4 inches and also has a companion dip dish which is 5-1/2 inches. A set of four ashtrays are part of this series and they measure 4 inches. All these serving pieces have the butler's head that serves as a handle. Value: chip dish—$75-$80; ashtrays—$45-$55 each.

Rock 'n Roll Kids salt & peppers: $65-$75 for set (from Dworkin Collection; photo by Van Blerck Photography).

ROCK 'N ROLL KIDS SALT & PEPPERS

Many collectors call this Rock 'n Roll salt & pepper shakers set Pixieware, but it is not. This duo is copyrighted 1959 and are not part of the Pixieware clan. Their heads are rounded and they sit on top of coil springs equipped with a heavy ring at bottom. These dancing dolls are 7 inches tall and a quick shake of your hand will make them rock and roll. Value: $65-$75 for the set.

Lovebirds Salt & Peppers: $35-$45 for set (from Dworkin Collection; photo by Van Blerck Photography).

LOVEBIRDS SALT & PEPPERS

This couple stares lovingly at each other and Holt-Howard named them "Lovebirds" salt & peppers. Each has a "Lift' n Listen" noise device built into its base. Salt and pepper can be added to the shakers through a plugged opening under their tails. The male has an "S" and the female a "P" on the side of their heads. The pair stands 3-1/2 inches and is signed and copyrighted 1960. Value: $35-$45 for the set.

Banana People Salt & Peppers: $25-$35 for set (from Dworkin Collection; photo by Van Blerck Photography).

BANANA PEOPLE SALT & PEPPERS

These banana fruit head salt & peppers are very small, measuring 2-1/4 inches. They are not signed, but they read "Japan." Value: $25-$35 for the set.

Poodle and cat salt & peppers: $30-$35 for set (from Dworkin Collection; photo by Van Blerck Photography).

POODLE AND CAT SALT & PEPPERS

This strange but adoring twosome is called "Puss and Poodle." These shakers are definitely a pair and were featured together in Holt-Howards catalog. The poodle is taller and stand 4-1/2 inches, while the cat stands 4 inches. The pair also appeared on top of a tall Holt-Howard ceramic gift box. Neither piece is signed, but both have the "HH" gold sticker. Value: $30-$35 for the set. There were also companion pieces in a variety of different-shaped snack trays which featured the two animals kissing (smack on the lips) on a striped background.

Bell Bottom Gobs salt & peppers: $45-$55 for set (from collection of and photo by Darline Comisky).

BELL BOTTOM GOBS SALT & PEPPERS

These "Bell Bottom Gobs" salt & pepper sailors are 4 inches tall and double as dinner bells. The shakers stare at each other and both have a bell clangor in their base. These sailors were featured in Holt-Howard's catalog. Value: $45-$55 for the set.

Bunnies salt & peppers in baskets: $25-$30 for the set (from Dworkin Collection; photo by Van Blerck Photography).

BUNNIES SALT & PEPPERS IN BASKETS

To date, I've seen these peeking bunnies salt & pepper sets in three different daisy color prints—pink, yellow and green. They are always identical, except for the color of their daisy flowers. The salt has four pouring holes in its head and the pepper has only two. The bunnies stand 3 inches high and are always found peeking out of their tiny baskets. These shakers are signed in green ink and copyrighted 1958. They were sold as a four-piece set comprised of two bunnies and two baskets. Value: $25-$30 for the set.

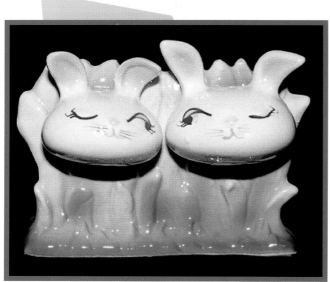

Winking' Wabbits set: $55-$65 (from collection of and photo by Darline Comisky).

WINKING' WABBITS SET

This three-piece set of "Winking' Wabbits" consists of a pair of salt & pepper shakers and a cabbage-patch napkin holder that is 4 inches by 3 inches. The rabbits wink at each other and hook onto the napkin holder to secure themselves in place. This set appeared in the 1958 Holt-Howard catalog. Value: $55-$65.

Chattercoons salt & peppers: $30-$35 for set (from Blair/Rodriguez Collection; photo by Mary Norman).

CHATTERCOONS SALT & PEPPERS

This set of "Chattercoons" salt & peppers is 4 inches tall and squeak when shaken. This duo was featured in Holt-Howard's 1958 catalog. Value: $30-$35 for the set.

Goose 'n Golden Egg salt & peppers: $30-$35 for set (from John Clay and Judy Shute collection; photo by Van Blerck Photography).

GOOSE 'N GOLDEN EGG SALT & PEPPERS

Holt-Howard advertised this two-piece set of 24k gold-on-white shakers as "folklore for the table." The goose has eight pouring holes that form an "S" for salt and the golden egg has eight pouring holes that form the "P" for pepper. This set is numbered "5285" and copyrighted 1958. Value: $30-$35 for the set.

Bobbing banks: cat, clown and lion—$125+ each (from Blair/Rodriguez Collection; photo by Mary Norman).

BOBBING COIN BANKS: CAT, CLOWN AND LION

These are some of the cutest banks ever created. Not only are their faces and designs adorable, but they are so reminiscent of the 1950s with their heads mounted on springs causing them to become (nodders) bobbing from movement or just from air currents. When money is deposited inside, the banks rock and roll back and forth! Some of the banks have the coin slot in back, while others have their slots in the front. These fun characters all stand about 6-1/2 inches and have a metal mechanism underneath to remove coins. The Brown Tabby has his coin slot in the front, while "Coin Clown" and "Dandy-Lion" have their coin slots in back. Dandy-Lion is not signed, but was featured in Holt-Howard's 1958 catalog. Coin Clown is signed and copyrighted 1958. Coin Kitty is not signed, but is believed to be Holt-Howard since no other companies copied these bobbing banks. Value: $125+ each.

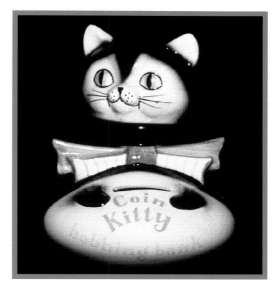

Bobbing coin bank: black and white kitty—$125+ (from collection of and photo by Darline Comisky).

Bobbing coin bank: blue clown—$125+ (from Blair/Rodriguez Collection; photo by Mary Norman).

BOBBING COIN BANK: BLUE CLOWN

This is another smiling clown with colored circles decorating his blue base. This coin clown's coin slot is located in his back; He was featured in Holt-Howard's 1958 catalog. Value: $125+.

BOBBING COIN BANK: BLACK & WHITE KITTY

This black and white beauty sports a big pink bow shaped exactly like the blue bow on the brown and white tabby. Her bow also matches the colors of her lettering, which reads "Bobbing Bank." This cat's coin slot is in front and she is signed and copyrighted 1958. Value: $125+.

Bobbing coin bank: pink cat—$125+ (from collection of and photo by Darline Comisky).

Bobbing coin bank: gray cat—$125+ (from collection of and photo by Darline Comisky).

BOBBING COIN BANK: PINK CAT

This colorful bobbing bank is 6-1/2 inches tall, her coin slot is in the back, and she is signed and copyrighted 1958. Of the four cat banks pictured here, this is the only one that has Siamese cat eyes, whereas all the others have rounded eyes. Value: $125+.

BOBBING COIN BANK: GRAY CAT

This gray tabby also wears the same blue bow as his brown and white tabby brother. His coin slot is in the front. This bank is not signed, but definitely related. Value: $125+

Pop-up candy jar: $225+ (from Dworkin Collection; photo by Van Blerck Photography).

Pop-Up Candy Jar

This "Just Take One" candy jar measures 6-1/4 inches tall (when closed with lid) and is 4 inches in diameter. When the lid is removed, a cute clown pops up to tell you, "Just Take One!" The clown is about 2 inches tall and his sign is 1-1/2 inches long. The piece is not signed, but has the black and gold "HH" sticker. Value: $225+.

Daisy 'Dorables, from left: cigarette holder—$55-$60; salt & peppers—$35-$45 for set; book-end wall-pocket planter—$35-$45; lipstick holder—$55-$60; two-section dish—$75-$85 (from Blair/Rodriguez Collection; photo by Mary Norman).

Daisy 'Dorables: Various Items

Holt-Howard called this series its "Pretty Lil' Pony Tail Princess." This set was designed primarily for dresser duty, except for the salt & pepper set. The little girl is always smelling a daisy flower which covers her nose and mouth. Here we see some of the pieces, including: 7-1/2-inch two-section dish ($75-$85); 4-inch diameter lipstick holder ($55-$60); 4-inch book-end/wall pocket planter ($35-$45); 3-1/2-inch salt & pepper set ($35-$45 for the set); 4-1/4-inch cigarette holder ($55-$60).

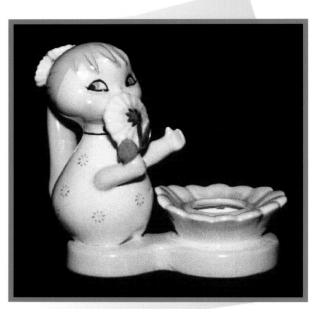

Daisy 'Dorables: candle holder—$30-$35 each (from collection of and photo by Darline Comisky).

Daisy 'Dorables: Candle Holder

This ponytail tot is one of a pair of candle holders that measures 4 inches. The ponytail girls are attached to a daisy flower candle holder. Value: $30-$35 each.

Daisy 'Dorables: bud vase—$65-$75 (from Blair/Rodriguez Collection; photo by Mary Norman).

Daisy 'Dorables: Bud Vase

This bud vase is 5-1/2 inches tall. The ponytail girl stands upright and has opening in her head for flowers or pencils. Copyrighted 1959. Value: $65-$75.

Daisy 'Dorables: covered box—$45-$50 (from Blair/Rodriguez Collection; photo by Mary Norman).

Daisy 'Dorables: Covered Box

This covered box measures 5 inches in diameter. The ponytail girl lies down on top of daisy flower lid. This storage box is for pins, buttons or powder. Value: $45-$50. Other pieces to this series include: 6-1/2-inch diameter covered box on which the ponytail girl stands upright on the daisy flower lid of jar ($50-$60); and a 5-1/2-inch diameter ashtray on which the ponytail girl stands upright on a daisy flower-shaped ashtray ($40-$50).

Li'L Old Lace: floral candelabra—$45-$55; candle holders—$20-$25 each (from Blair/Rodriguez Collection; photo by Mary Norman).

Li'L Old Lace: Floral Candelabra and Candle Holders

Many collectors refer to these pieces as "The Granny" collection, but they are actually called "Li'L Old Lace." They were referred to by Holt-Howard in advertising as "Gray but gay—naughty but nice." These pieces were offered in either lavender or blue and all pieces were available in these two colors. The "Li'L Old Lace" collection was featured in Holt-Howard's 1960 catalog. The floral candelabra in the middle serves two functions: a dual candle holder and a stem tender. The stem tender is located behind grandma and serves as a holder for floral arrangements; it is copyrighted 1959. The candle holders'

bonnet bases are also vases which can be filled with flowers. There are holes around granny's bonnet to insert cut flowers. The pieces to this set are 3-1/2 inches high. Value: floral candelabra—$45-$55; candle holders—$20-$25 each.

Li'L Old Lace: card holder/money hat—$45-$55 (from Blair/Rodriguez Collection; photo by Mary Norman).

Li'L Old Lace: Card Holder/Money Hat

This granny card holder is large enough to accommodate gambling cards, while holding money in her hat! This piece stands 5 inches high. Value: $45-$55.

Li'L Old Lace: ashtray—$45-$55 (from collection of and photo by Chris Mahlock).

Li'L Old Lace: Ashtray

Granny seems to be in quite a predicament in this fun-making ashtray, which stands 5-1/2 inches high. Value: $45-$55.

Li'L Old Lace: magnet salt & peppers—$35-$45 (from Blair/Rodriguez Collection; photo by Mary Norman).

Li'L Old Lace: Magnet Salt & Peppers

Holt-Howard referred to this salt & pepper shaker duo as "Hammy Grannies." The grannies are dancing with glasses in their hands, while a pair of magnets (attached to their heads) helps hold them up! These shakers stand 3-3/4 inches tall. Value: $35-$45.

Cow salt & peppers: $30-$40 for set (from Blair/Rodriguez Collection; photo by Mary Norman).

Cow Salt & Peppers

Two sets of these cow salt & peppers were made. One set is called "Moo Cow," since it has a voice mechanism in it. The other set is called "Smacking Boss & Bossie," and it does not apparently have the "moo" mechanism. Both sets are 3-1/4 inches tall and are very similar; however, the moo-cow's tongue is licking her lips in one set, while "Bossy" just has an opened mouth in another set. These shakers were featured in the 1958 catalog. Value: $30-$40 for set.

Cow sugar shaker and milk pitcher: $65-$75 for set (from the collection of and photo by Donna and Steve Wisnewski).

Cow Sugar Shaker and Milk Pitcher

This adorable couple is quite unique for a sugar and creamer set. The cow sugar and creamer are extra large (which saves having to fill them often). Each stands 4-1/2 inches. The sugar is unique since the sugar pours out of the 13 holes in the back of her head and she has a cork in her base to hold in contents. The sugar cow's creamer companion is yawning and has a handle attached to his back for pouring out cream. This cute duo was sold as a set and is copyrighted 1958. Value: $65-$75 for the set. There's one more piece to this cow series—an 8-ounce cow tumbler that makes a "moo" sound when turned over. This piece was featured in the 1958 catalog and has a value of $30-$35.

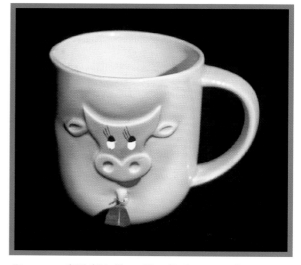

Cow mug: $15-$20 (from Blair/Rodriguez Collection; photo by Mary Norman).

Cow Mug

This comical 10-ounce cow mug has a "ring for refill" cow bell attached. Value: $15-$20.

Bull mug: $15-$20 (from Blair/Rodriguez Collection; photo by Mary Norman).

BULL MUG

This cute bull is reminiscent of Ferdinand the bull smelling flowers. This cute mug is copyrighted 1961. Value: $15-$20.

Ice cream sundae sets: $55-$65 for each (from Dworkin Collection; photo by Van Blerck Photography).

ICE CREAM SUNDAE SETS

Each one of these sundae servers is comprised of three pieces—a pitcher type base, the stackable condiment jar and the jar's lid. The two servers that make up this set are chocolate and strawberries and butterscotch and nuts. The servers are styled in ice cream colors and help make easy fixing for ice cream sundaes and banana splits. Each server stands 5-1/2 inches tall and both pieces are copyrighted 1959. Value: $55-$65 for each set.

Hunter and fisherman ashtrays: $95-$110 each (from Blair/Rodriguez Collection; photo by Mary Norman).

HUNTER AND FISHERMAN IMAGE ASHTRAYS

These pieces are known as "image ashtrays" since the bottom portion serves as the ashtray while smoke curls through their mouths and ears. Here we have the hunter with his rifle and the fisherman holding his fishing rod. Both pieces stand 5-1/4 inches and are copyrighted 1961. Value: $95-$110 each.

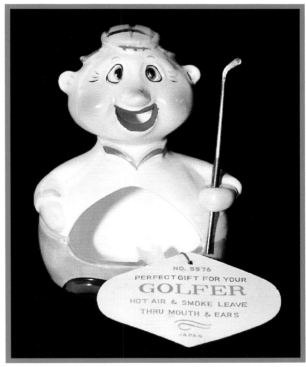

Golfer ashtray: $95-$110 (from collection of and photo by Darline Comisky).

GOLFER IMAGE ASHTRAY

This smiling sportsman is the third party to the Image Ashtrays. The golfer, 5-1/4 inches and copyrighted 1961, is complete only when he holds his golf club. Value: $95-$110.

Bride & groom candle holders and rings: $35-$45 for set (from Dworkin Collection; photo by Van Blerck Photography).

BRIDE & GROOM CANDLE HOLDERS AND RINGS

These bride and groom candle holders stand 4 inches tall. The bride wears an actual real veil! The candle holders are attached and located behind them. This couple was sold as a four-piece set complete with matching gold and white wedding bell candle rings. Both pieces have the "HH" label. Value: $35-$45 for the set.

New Year's Eve candle rings: $35-$45 for set (from Blair/Rodriguez Collection; photo by Mary Norman).

NEW YEAR'S EVE CANDLE RINGS

These miniature New Year's Eve candle rings are 1-1/2 inches and are just a sampling of the many holiday candle rings that Holt-Howard created. Value: $35-$45 for the set.

Bluebird candle rings—$35-$45 for set; complete set with bases—$75-$85 (from collection of and photo by Darline Comisky).

BLUEBIRD CANDLE RINGS AND BASES

Bluebird candle rings are 1-1/2 inches and come with candle holder vases that are 3-1/2 inches. This four-piece set is copyrighted 1959. Value: candle rings—$35-$45 for the set; complete set with bases—$75-$85.

Ballerina candle rings—$35-$45 for set; complete set with bases—$75-$85 (from collection of and photo by Darline Comisky).

BALLERINA CANDLE RINGS

Ballerina candle rings are 4 inches and their matching bases are 3-1/2 inches. This four-piece set was offered in pink, blue or yellow and is copyrighted 1958. Value: candle rings—$35-$45 for the set; complete set with bases—$75-$85.

White Pixie candle climbers—$35-$45; complete set with bases— $75-$85 (from Dworkin Collection; photo by Van Blerck Photography).

WHITE PIXIE CANDLE CLIMBERS

These Pixie candle climbers are 3 inches. They were originally sold with the option of purchasing them as a pair, with or without their matching rounded candle holder bases. These pixies are not signed, but were featured in the 1958 Holt-Howard catalog. Holt-Howard was the first company to create candle climbers or "sliders" and manufactured a large selection of them in the shape of flowers, butterflies, birds, cherubs and Easter and Christmas figures. Value: climbers—$35-$45; complete set with bases—$75-$85.

Honey Bunnies climbers—$35-$45; complete set with bases— $75-$85 (from Blair/Rodriguez Collection; photo by Mary Norman).

HONEY BUNNIES CANDLE CLIMBERS

Holt-Howard named these Easter candle delights, "Honey Bunny Candle Climbers." The pair is 3-1/2 inches and fits all standard candles. This duo appeared in the Easter section of Holt-Howard's 1958 catalog. Value: climbers—$35-$45; complete set with bases—$75-$85.

Feathered chicks climbers—$35-$45; complete set with bases— $75-$85 (from collection of and photo by Darline Comisky).

FEATHERED CHICKS CANDLE CLIMBERS

Feather chicks candle climbers are 2-3/4 inches tall and are climbing up the candle after hatching out of their 3-1/2 inch cracked egg-shaped floral vase bases. This is a four-piece set; however, the chicks could have been purchased separately. This set is copyrighted 1958. Value: climbers—$35-$45; complete set with bases—$75-$85.

Totem pole rabbits and chicks: $35-$40 each (from Blair/Rodriguez Collection; photo by Mary Norman).

TOTEM POLE RABBITS AND CHICKS

The rabbits and chicks totem-pole candle holders are 8 inches high. Each holds an array of three, 1/2-inch candles. These rabbits and chicks are perched one atop the other and have the "HH" sticker. These pieces were individually boxed and not sold as a pair. They were featured in the 1958 catalog. Value: $35-$40 each.

Rabbit candle holders: $30-$35 for pair (from Blair/Rodriguez Collection; photo by Mary Norman).

RABBIT CANDLE HOLDERS

One of the rabbit candle holders has a blue underplate for his candle, while his mate has a pink underplate. Value: $30-$35 for the pair.

Large cat bank: $55-$60 (from Blair/Rodriguez Collection; photo by Mary Norman).

LARGE CAT BANK

Although this cat is not part of the Cozy Kitten series, she has her own personality. This tabby has a coin slot to deposit money and serves as a very decorative bank. Value: $55-$60.

Giraffe hot plate: $40-$50 (from Blair/Rodriguez Collection; photo by Mary Norman).

Horse hot plate: $40-$50 (from collection of and photo by Darline Comisky).

Puppy hot plate: $40-$50 (from collection of and photo by Darline Comisky).

ANIMAL HOT PLATES: GIRAFFE, HORSE & PUPPY

The giraffe (8 inches by 5 inches), horse (9 inches by 5 inches) and puppy (8 inches by 4 inches) hot plates were used for children's meals. Each has a water vent for hot water (the tail of each animal has a cork attached). Holt-Howard called these dish animals "fun mates for hot food and happy eating." Value: $40-$50 each.

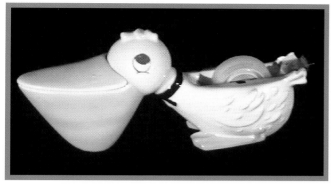

Pelican Pete: $70-$80 (from Blair/Rodriguez Collection; photo by Mary Norman).

Pelican Pete with lid of beak removed (from collection of and photo by Hall/Glascock).

PELICAN PETE DESK ACCESSORY

"Pelican Pete" is 8-3/4 inches long and about 4 inches high. He is a tape dispenser that holds the standard 800 inches of scotch tape. The upper portion of Pete's large beak is removable and the inside serves as a storage compartment for clips, tacks, stamps and so on. Pete is copyrighted 1958. Value: $70-$80.

Chickadee tape dispenser, gold and white: $70-$80 (from Dworkin Collection; photo by Van Blerck Photography).

Chickadee tape dispenser, turquoise and walnut: $70-$80 (from Blair/Rodriguez Collection; photo by Mary Norman).

CHICKADEE SHARPEN TAPE TOTES

These are two versions of Holt-Howard's "Chickadee Sharpen Tape Tote." Each is equipped with a pencil sharpener in his mouth and a tape dispenser capable of holding the standard 800 inches of scotch tape. One piece was issued in gold and white and the other in turquoise and walnut. These dispenser's heads are removable to dispose of pencil shavings. They are 5 inches long and copyrighted 1958. Value: $70-$80 each.

There was also a companion piece to this set called "Chickadee Desk Set" (5 inches by 8 inches). It featured the same chickadee head perched in the center of a compartmentalized ceramic desk organizer that stood on a brass revolving stand. Companion pieces to this series included: chickadee clips 2 inches long (a four-piece set that contained two pairs per set). They were ceramic birds with positive action clips attached, and they came in assorted colors.

Chickadee sharpener: $65-$75 for set (from collection of and photo by Darline Comisky).

CHICKADEE SHARPEN HOLD 'EM SET

This chickadee set is 4 inches high. One chickadee sharpens pencils while his companion holds them. The sharpener chickadee originally came with a pair of eye glasses that sat on top of his beak. Value: $65-$75 for the set.

Cock-A-Doodle sharpener: $50-$60 for set (from Blair/Rodriguez Collection; photo by Mary Norman).

COCK-A-DOODLE SHARPEN HOLD 'EM SET

This sharpener set is 6 inches high; one bird has a pencil sharpener mouth, while his companion is a pencil holder. Value: $50-$60 for the set.

Professor Perch sharpener: $65-$75 for set (from Blair/Rodriguez Collection; photo by Mary Norman).

PROFESSOR PERCH SHARPEN HOLD 'EM SET

Professor Perch is also a two-piece set that sharpens and stores pencils and is 2-1/2 inches tall. Value: $65-$75 for the set.

Pheasant letter holder, front view: $60-$70 (from collection of and photo by Darline Comisky).

Pheasant letter holder, side view (Darline Comisky).

PHEASANT LETTER HOLDER

This pheasant letter holder also serves as a memo tender. This piece has a gleaming brass coil to hold letters and is 4-1/2 inches tall. Value: $60-$70. Holt-Howard made a series of these mallards and pheasants desk accessories. Among them were: pheasant pencil sharpener and holder ($65-$75 for the set); dual pheasant desk-set pen holder ($70-$80 for the set); mallard desk caddy ($75-$85); various bookends ($35-$45 each); planters and wall pockets ($35-$45 each); mallards or pheasants in flight (sets of three) wall pockets ($45-$55 per set).

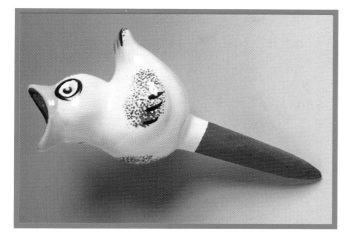

Weekend Willie plant waterer: $25-$35 (from Dworkin Collection; photo by Van Blerck Photography).

BIRD PLANT WATERER: "WEEKEND WILLIE"

"Weekend Willie" was probably the very first whimsical, ceramic plant-waterer with a head created by any company. Although tube-type plant waterers were in existence 40 years ago, Holt-Howard was the first company to incorporate a ceramic-head that holds water and gradually releases the water through a porous non glazed cone. Just fill Willie's head with water and he'll take care of your plant in your absence. Willie was made in different colors and was promoted and introduced by B. Altman & Co. Willie is 6 inches long. Value: $25-$35.

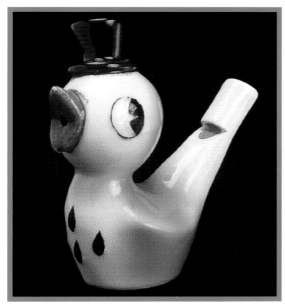

Willie Warbler bird call: $35-$40 (from John Clay and Judy Shute Collection; photo by Van Blerck Photography).

WILLIE WARBLER BIRD CALL

Just add water to "Willie Warbler," blow through his tail and the warbles of your favorite birds are easily copied. Flocks of birds will also gather around you. Willie Warbler is 2-1/2 inches and was featured in Holt-Howard's 1958 catalog. Value: $35-$40.

Sunbonnet Miss napkin doll, pink: $70-$80 (from Blair/Rodriguez Collection; photo by Mary Norman).

Sunbonnet Miss napkin doll, yellow: $70-$80 (from collection of and photo by Bobbie and Alan Bryson).

SUNBONNET MISS NAPKIN DOLL

The Sunbonnet Miss napkin holder doll is 5 inches tall and is also a candle holder. Napkins can be placed within the openings of her dress. She's a real party perker and comes in three different poses and colors—pink, blue or yellow. Originally, this napkin doll was offered with eight rice paper napkins and color coordinated candles and appeared in Holt-Howard's 1958 catalog. Value: $70-$80 each.

Blue Girl candle holder: $25-$35 (from Dworkin Collection; photo by Van Blerck Photography).

BLUE GIRL CANDLE HOLDER

This "Candle Miss" candle holder is 4-1/2 inches high and was offered in three different colors—blue, pink and yellow. This candle holder was featured in Holt-Howard's 1958 catalog. Value: $25-$35 each.

Slick Chick egg cups: $50-$60 for set (from Dworkin Collection; photo by Van Blerck Photography).

SLICK CHICK EGG CUPS SALT AND PEPPERS

Holt-Howard named this duo "Slick Chick Egg Cups." The chicks are salt & pepper shakers, with gold letters "S" and "P" posted on top of their heads. These chicks are removable from their egg cup bases and also serve as thermal tops to keep eggs warm. This set stands 4 inches tall and was sold as a four-piece set. Value: $50-$60 for the set.

Peepin' Tom & Tweetie salt and peppers: $30-$40 for set (from Blair/Rodriguez Collection; photo by Mary Norman).

PEEPIN' TOM & TWEETIE SALT AND PEPPERS

This salt & pepper set is but a small part of the "Peepin' Tom & Tweetie" collection that Holt-Howard created. The salt & peppers actually peep when shaken and are 4-1/2 inches tall. Value: $30-$40 for the set.

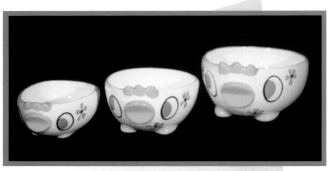

Peepin' Tom & Tweetie stackables: $30-$35 for set (from Blair/Rodriguez Collection; photo by Mary Norman).

PEEPIN' TOM & TWEETIE STACKABLES

This three-piece set of Peepin' Tom & Tweetie trays is comprised of three small condiment holders that are piggyback stackable. This trio of trays are great for condiments, sauces, jams or nuts. This trio measures 3-1/4 inches, 4 inches and 4-1/2 inches long. Value: $30-$35 for the three-piece set.

Also included in this set were: 4-inch egg cups with thermal salt & pepper tops to keep eggs warm ($55-$60 for set); 3-1/4-inch candle holders ($35-$40); 7-inch covered butter dish ($60-$70); 4-1/2-inch sugar & creamer with the top of the sugar's head having a built-in saccharin server that holds 100 tablets ($65-$75); 4-1/2-inch, three-piece candle food-warmer set for butter, sauces or gravy with the bird's head holding the liquids to be warmed and the base holding a 10-hour candle ($55-$65).

Pony Pal lamp: $65-$75 (from Blair/Rodriguez Collection; photo by Mary Norman).

PONY PAL LAMP

The night-lamp pony pal is 6 inches tall and originally came with a blue lamp on the pony's back. Other pieces to this set included a pair of 6-inch book ends, 5-1/4-inch penny bank and a 4-inch pin cushion/button box. Lamp's value: $65-$75.

Market Piggy: $70-$80 (from collection of and photo by Darline Comisky).

MARKET PIGGY DESK ORGANIZER

Holt-Howard advertised this Market Piggy as "some little piggies have none, but this little piggy has everything—string holder, pad, ball pen with calendar and a pair of fine Keentempre scissors." This organizer is 6 inches by 8 inches and was featured in Holt-Howard's 1958 catalog. The Market Piggy also had a companion piggy piece that was a 6-inch long Citronella candle holder that came with a 15-hour Citronella candle. Market Piggy value: $70-$80.

Citronella Chickadee Hanger

This Citronella chickadee is 6 inches long and originally included a 15-hour Citronella candle. This

Citronella chickadee hanger: $45-$50 (from Blair/Rodriguez Collection; photo by Mary Norman).

piece can be hung on a tree or set on a table. Her ceramic finish is called "Stippletex." This chickadee hanger was featured in the 1958 catalog. Value: $45-$50.

White bull planter: $25-$35 (from Blair/Rodriguez Collection; photo by Mary Norman).

WHITE BULL PLANTER

Although this bull is not really whimsical, he was quite the fad in his hay day. He has a built-in planter to accommodate a house plant. Value: $25-$35.

Minnie & Moby: powder jar and pill box—$45-$55 each (from collection of and photo by Evan Pazol).

MINNIE & MOBY: POWDER JAR AND PILL BOX

Holt-Howard came out with a series of little kid-like mermaids called Minnie & Moby and referred to them as "mer-moppets." Minnie & Moby adorned a host of ceramic items for the bath and bedroom. These pieces were colored sea blue and yellow on white.

This is a 3-inch diameter pill box with Moby perched on top of the jar's lid. The matching twin powder jar is 3 inches with Minnie perched on top. Value $45-$55 each.

Minnie cotton ball dispenser—$65-$75 (from collection of and photo by Hall/Glascock).

Minnie Cotton Ball Dispenser

Here we see Minnie pulling at the cotton while perched atop of the cotton ball dispenser which measures 4-1/2 inches high by 2-3/4 inches wide. This piece is copyrighted 1959. Value: $65-$75.

Moby ashtray—$45-$55 (from collection of and photo by Evan Pazol).

Moby Ashtray

This Moby ashtray is 4 inches and there's a recess behind Moby to hold a book of matches. Value: $45-$55.

Moby matchbox—$55-$65 (from collection of and photo by Evan Pazol).

Moby Match Box

This Moby matchbox measures 5 inches. Value: $55-$65.

Minnie & Moby: sea horse wall planters—$75-$85 each (from collection of and photo by Evan Pazol).

Minnie & Moby: Sea Horse Wall Planters

These are sea horse wall planters, 6-3/4 inches, with Minnie and Moby ridding the sea horses. These two were sold as a set and were in Holt-Howard's 1958 catalog. Value: $75-$85 each.

Other pieces in the Minnie & Moby set include: 4-1/2-inch Minnie soap dish that was sold with an 8-ounce tumbler as a two piece set ($50-$60, with original tumbler); 4-1/2-inch Minnie & Moby atomizer set ($65-$75 each); 4-3/4-inch nail file and 5-inch brush set ($25-$35 each); 7-1/4-inch Minnie & Moby bath bottles ($65-$75 each).

Dresser Dollie: stackable organizer—$40-$50 (from collection of and photo by Chris Mahlock).

DRESSER DOLLIE: STACKABLE ORGANIZER

A cute Dresser Dollie perches atop a stackable organizer. It measures 5 inches high and is comprised of three sections for storage of pins and clips. The top piece has a built-in tape measure. Value: $40-$50.

Dresser Dollie: atomizer—$65-$75 (from collection of and photo by Chris Mahlock).

DRESSER DOLLIE: ATOMIZER

This Dresser Dollie atomizer (with funnel) is 4-1/2 inches tall. There are two more cylindrical storage container pieces to this set, measuring 4-1/2 inches and 2-1/2 inches. These containers also have the Dresser

Dollies perched on top of their lids. The Dresser Dollies set was featured in Holt-Howard's 1958 catalog. Value (atomizer): $65-$75.

Tiger salt & peppers: $15-$20 for set (from Dworkin Collection; photo by Van Blerck Photography).

TIGER SALT & PEPPERS

These smiling tigers are 3-1/2 inches high and are part of the Holt-Howard tiger cookie jar set, which also includes mugs and a napkin holder. The tiger set is a later Holt-Howard product of the 1970s. Value: (shakers) $15-$20 for the set.

Tea Time Tillie: $35-$45 (from collection of and photo by Deborah Howard).

TEA TIME TILLIE

Tea Time Tillie is a bird tea bag (or loose tea) holder. Just pour hot water through Tillie and she will process your tea. Tillie rests on top of her matching nest which catches the tea drippings. Value: $35-$45.

Super Scooper: jam 'n jelly—$40-$50 (from Blair/Rodriguez Collection; photo by Mary Norman).

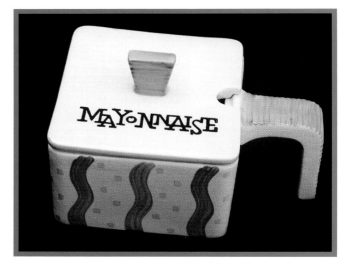

Super Scooper: mayonnaise—$40-$50 (from collection of and photo by Darline Comisky).

Super Scooper: hot stuff—$40-$50 (from John Clay and Judy Shute Collection; photo by Van Blerck Photography).

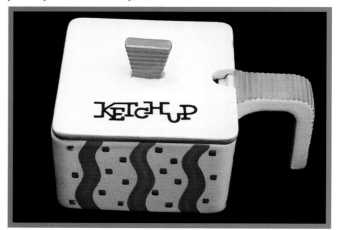

Super Scooper: ketchup—$40-$50 (from collection of and photo by Darline Comisky).

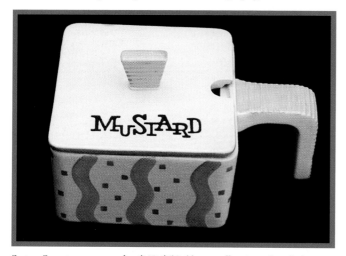

Super Scooper: mustard—$40-$50 (from collection of and photo by Darline Comisky).

Super Scooper: pickles—$40-$50 (from collection of and photo by Darline Comisky).

SUPER SCOOPERS

These condiment jars are called "Super Scoopers." Their design was inspired by early American sugar scoops. These condiments are 6 inches and ideal for transporting condiments anywhere. Although sold individually, each is considered a three-piece set (with lid and spoon). This is the complete set of six pieces including: mustard, ketchup, mayonnaise, jam 'n jelly, pickles and hot stuff. Value: $40-$50 each.

Welcome to the world of fantasy! For any of us that grew up believing in Santa Claus and the magic of Christmas, Holt-Howard has captured these memories for us forever in their wonderful ceramics, and other Christmas related gift wares. Holt-Howard always stated that decorations say welcome so well, and they always referred to Santa Claus as the North Pole's first citizen always eager to spice and spruce up your holiday season.

There was always something magical about the way that Holt-Howard designed their Santas, it only takes a quick glance at a flea market or collectible show to recognize the great facial expressions on the Santa's, and to realize immediately that the piece is a Holt-Howard collectible. Whenever Holt-Howard sat down at their drawing board to develop a new holiday line, they always created an entirely different and exciting Santa. As mentioned earlier, many of the Santa mugs in this chapter were so successful

and popular that they paved the way for the creation of the coffee mug as we know it today. Some of these mugs were also filled with holiday candles and sold as "muglites" candle holders.

But it wasn't only the Santas that were super stars. When it came to Christmas giftwares, Holt-Howard encompassed an unforgettable array of not only decorative, but extremely serviceable holiday collectibles. Everything from its small salt and pepper shakers to its large pitchers and cookie jars would always bring a smile to any holiday shopper's face. Although Holt-Howard created numerous paper, cardboard, foil, wood and other material Christmas decorations, this chapter will be primarily dedicated to the company's ceramic creations. This chapter represents a sampling of so many of the great Christmas collectibles by Holt-Howard, but certainly enough to capture the true essence of this most creative company.

Merry Whiskers: beverage set: $50-$60 for set (from Dworkin Collection; photo by Van Blerck Photography).

Winking Santa: beverage set: $50-$60 for set (from Dworkin Collection; photo by Van Blerck Photography).

MERRY WHISKERS: BEVERAGE SET

Holt-Howard introduced a variety of Santa Claus pitchers, mugs and tumblers for all kinds of holiday entertaining. All the Santas were different, and each series was offered with numerous related giftware items. This beverage set was named "Merry Whiskers" and consisted of a 36-ounce pitcher and six, 4-1/2-ounce mugs. The pitcher was also sold separately. All pieces are copyrighted 1959. Value: $50-$60 for the set.

WINKING SANTA: BEVERAGE SET

Holt-Howard named this beverage set the "Winking Santa," and it was offered with other matching pieces. This seven-piece set, copyrighted 1960, has a 32-ounce pitcher and comes with six, 6-ounce mugs. Even though this was sold as a seven-piece set, the pitcher could be purchased separately, as well as the mugs (four to a box). Value: $50-$60 for the set.

Cloud Santa: beverage set—$50-$60; salt & peppers—$20-$25 for set (from Dworkin Collection; photo by Van Blerck Photography).

CLOUD SANTA: BEVERAGE SET & SALT & PEPPERS

I've always referred to this set as the "Cloud Santa" because of his cloud-shaped beard. This set is unique since it was sold with tumblers instead of mugs. The cloud Santa is copyrighted 1967. One shaker of the matching salt & pepper set is pictured here. Value: beverage set—$50-$60; salt & peppers—$20-$25 for the set.

Winking Santa: beverage set—$50-$60 for set (from Dworkin Collection; photo by Van Blerck Photography).

WINKING SANTA: BEVERAGE SET

This green-eyed Winking Santa beverage set was issued with a 44-ounce pitcher and six, 6-ounce mugs. There was also a 24-ounce matching pitcher. The set is copyrighted 1959 and contains many other green-eyed Winking Santa matching pieces. Value: $50-$60 for the set.

Winking Santa: punch bowl set—$115-$125 (from Dworkin Collection; photo by Van Blerck Photography).

Winking Santa: Punch Bowl Set

This 10-piece "Jolly Mr. Claus" set has a 3-quart punch bowl, eight, 6-ounce mugs and candy cane-striped ladle. Although the Santa punch bowl has both eyes open, he is part of the Winking Santa series, since all his mugs are winkers. Some of the mugs wink to the right and others to the left. This set is copyrighted 1962 and was made in limited numbers. Value: 10-piece set with ladle—$115-$125.

Winking Santa: pitcher—$45-$55 for set (from Dworkin Collection; photo by Van Blerck Photography).

WINKING SANTA: EGG NOG PITCHER AND NUTMEG SHAKER

This Winking Santa 40-ounce egg nog pitcher and 4-1/2-inch high nutmeg shaker were sold as a set with a

Winking Santa: nutmeg shaker—$45-$55 for set (from collection of and photo by Darline Comisky).

copyright of 1960. This squat pitcher also came in a 32-ounce size and was sold separately. Value: $45-$55 for the set.

Starry-Eyed Santa: pitcher—$25-$35; mug—$8-$10 (from Blair/Rodriguez collection; photo by Mary Norman).

STARRY-EYED SANTA: PITCHER AND MUG

Holt-Howard named this series its "Starry-Eyed Santa." Pictured is a 16-ounce pitcher and matching mug. All the Santas in this series have daisy-shaped eyes that take on a star-like appearance. Value: pitcher—$25-$35; mug—$8-$10.

Starry-Eyed Santa: pitcher—$30-$40; sweet dish—$20-$25; ashtray—$35-$40 (from Blair/Rodriguez collection; photo by Mary Norman).

STARRY-EYED SANTA: PITCHER, SWEET DISH AND ASHTRAY

This is the large 44-ounce Starry-Eyed Santa pitcher accompanied by a matching "Santa Sweet Tray." These sweet trays were made in three different sizes: 4 inches, 5-1/2 inches and 7 inches. Also pictured is a Santa cigarette holder/ashtray combination. Value: pitcher—$30-$40; sweet dish—$20-$25; ashtray—$35-$40.

Starry-Eyed Santa: salt & peppers—$25-$30 for set; mug—$10-$15 each (from the collection of and photo by Darline Comisky).

STARRY-EYED SANTA: SALT & PEPPERS WITH MUG

Here is a set of Starry-Eyed Santa salt & peppers and a straight-handled 8-ounce egg nog (or hot chocolate) stackable mug. The stackable mugs are copyrighted 1959. Value: salt & peppers—$25-$30 for the set; mug—$10-$15 each.

Starry-Eyed Santa: chip & cheese dish: $35-$40 (from Donna and Steve Wisnewski Collection; photo by Steve Wisnewski).

STARRY-EYED SANTA: CHIP & CHEESE DISH

The Starry-Eyed Santa chip & cheese dish is decorated with lots of gold and is 12 inches long. It is copyrighted 1960. Value: $35-$40.

Starry-Eyed Santa: planter/candle holder—$30-$35 (from Dworkin Collection; photo by Van Blerck Photography).

STARRY-EYED SANTA: PLANTER/CANDLE HOLDER

This unique Starry-Eyed Santa piece is not only a planter, but also a candle holder. Santa extends his arms holding a daisy wreath which has a 1-inch opening for a large holiday candle. Santa's bell on the tip of his cap jingles every time he is touched. This combination planter/candle holder is 6 inches tall, signed Holt-Howard and numbered 6268. Value: $30-$35.

Winking Santa: stackable salt & peppers—$30-$35 for set (from Dworkin Collection; photo by Van Blerck Photography).

WINKING SANTA: STACKABLE SALT & PEPPERS

Stackable green-eyed Winking Santa salt & peppers stand 5-1/2 inches tall. He has the "S" on his cap for salt, the "P" on his arm for pepper and is copyrighted 1959. Value: $30-$35 for the set.

Winking Santa: stackable cream & sugar—$30-$35 for set (from Dworkin Collection; photo by Van Blerck Photography).

WINKING SANTA: STACKABLE CREAM & SUGAR

Stackable green-eyed Winking Santa creamer & sugar set stand 4-1/2 inches tall and is copyrighted 1959. Value: $30-$35 for the set.

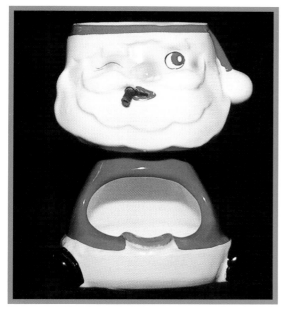

Winking Santa: ashtray—$40-$50 (from collection of and photo by Darline Comisky).

WINKING SANTA: ASHTRAY

The top of this green-eyed Winking Santa's head holds cigarettes, while his stomach serves as an ashtray. This Santa stands 5 inches tall, 3 inches wide and is copyrighted 1959. Value: $40-$50.

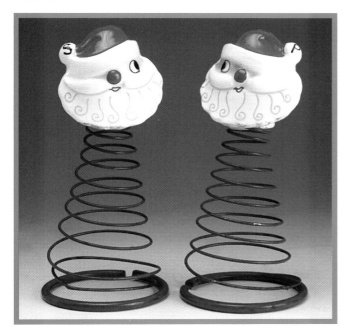

Rock 'n Roll Santa salt & peppers: $55-$65 for set (from Dworkin Collection; photo by Van Blerck Photography).

ROCK 'N ROLL SANTAS SALT & PEPPERS

Rock 'n Roll Santas salt & peppers wink at each other and dance back and forth the moment they are touched. Each Santa's cap designates an "S" or "P" to identify their contents. The duo are about 5-1/2 inches tall on their festive red springs and are copyrighted 1959. Value: $55-$65 for the set.

Winking Santa: salt & peppers—$30-$35 for set (from Dworkin Collection; photo by Van Blerck Photography).

WINKING SANTA: SALT & PEPPERS

These Winking Santa salt & peppers stand 5 inches high and each Santa sports a large gold button designating "P" or "S" to identify his contents. The pair is copyrighted 1960. Value: $30-$35 for the set.

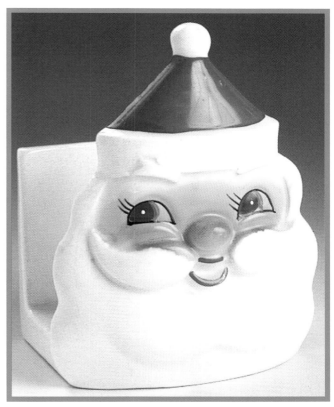

Santa napkin holder: $20-$25 (from Dworkin Collection; photo by Van Blerck Photography).

SANTA NAPKIN HOLDER

This Santa napkin holder is 4 inches high and is copyrighted 1964. Value: $20-$25.

Santa trays: $20-$25 each (from Dworkin Collection; photo by Van Blerck Photography).

SANTA TRAYS

These are two different sizes of Santa trays: one is 7-3/4 inches long and copyrighted 1962; the other is 8 inches and copyrighted 1961. The reason for these two copyright dates and different sizes is that each piece was probably manufactured at a different factory in Japan and created from two different molds. Value: $20-$25 each.

Santa pop-up candy jar: $150+ (from Dworkin Collection; photo by Van Blerck Photography).

SANTA POP-UP CANDY JAR

This candy jar has a lid that, when removed, up pops a cute little Santa to remind you to "Just Take One." This jar measures 6-1/2 inches high, and is not copyrighted, but has a rectangular "HH" foil sticker. This candy jar was featured with many other 1960 Christmas collectibles in Holt-Howard's holiday catalog. Value: $150+.

Santa pop-up cookie jar: $150+ (from collection of and photo by Darline Comisky).

SANTA POP-UP COOKIE JAR

This is another version of the Santa pop-up candy jar, but this one is for cookies. It also stands 6-1/2 inches tall. Value: $150+.

Winking Santa: sugar & creamer—$30-$40 for set (from Dworkin Collection; photo by Van Blerck Photography).

WINKING SANTA: SUGAR & CREAMER

The sugar is 4-3/4 inches tall and the creamer 3 inches tall. Sugar Santa has an opening in his lid to insert a spoon. Both pieces are copyrighted 1960. Value: $30-$40 for the set.

Santa candle holder: $15-$20 (from collection of and photo by Darline Comisky).

SANTA CANDLE HOLDER

This Santa night-light chamber candle holder is 2 inches high, with a 5-1/2-inch saucer. This night light holds a large candle and is copyrighted 1959. Value: $15-$20.

Winking Santa: party favors—$18-$20 for set (from Dworkin Collection; photo by Van Blerck Photography).

WINKING SANTA: PARTY FAVORS

This set of six miniature mugs can be used as party favors to hold cigarettes, flowers and candy or to use as a shot glass. Each mug holds 1-1/2 ounces. Three of the Santas' wink to the left and the other three to the right. Value: $18-$20 for the set.

Snowbird tree: $25-$35 (from collection of and photo by Darline Comisky).

SNOWBIRD TREE

This snowbird tree has sockets behind tree to insert 1/2-inch candles. The Christmas tree stands 8-3/4 inches tall and is copyrighted 1959. Value: $25-$35.

Noel candle holder: $15-$20 (from Dworkin Collection; photo by Van Blerck Photography).

Winking Santa: tiny favors—$2 each (from Dworkin Collection; photo by Van Blerck Photography).

NOEL CANDLE HOLDER

Santa places a cheery letter "O" into this noel candle holder to make it complete. This holiday candle holder is 9 inches long, 3 inches high, and copyrighted 1959. Value: $15-$20.

WINKING SANTA: TINY FAVORS

These green-eyed Santa favors are miniature, holding about 1-1/2 ounces. Each stares in a different direction and both are copyrighted 1959. Value: $2 each.

S.S. Noel set: $85-$95 with flag (from Dworkin Collection; photo by Van Blerck Photography).

S.S. NOEL SET

The S.S. Noel ship is fully staffed with Santa and his first-mate snowman. Santa has the "S" for salt on his hat; the snowman has "P" for pepper. The center opening smokestack appears to be a candle holder. This piece is missing a tiny flag that that inserts in the back of the ship that reads "Noel." This piece measures 5-1/2 inches long and 3-1/2 inches high and is copyrighted 1959. Value: $85-$95 (set with flag).

S.S. Noel candle holders: $25-$30 for set (from Dworkin Collection; photo by Van Blerck Photography).

S.S. NOEL CANDLE HOLDERS

S.S. Noel candle holders have two Santas searching for Christmas Island. They measure 2-3/4 inches and are copyrighted 1959. Value: $25-$30 for the set.

Girl candle holder: $12-$18 (from Dworkin Collection; photo by Van Blerck Photography).

GIRL CANDLE HOLDER

This Christmas miss candle holder is 3-1/2 inches tall and all stacked up with gifts. She is copyrighted 1959. Value: $12-$18.

My Fair Lady head vase: $50-$55 (from Dworkin Collection; photo by Van Blerck Photography).

MY FAIR LADY HEAD VASE

This piece is named "My Fair Lady" and is fully decorated with Christmas holly. When I first purchased her, I thought that she was only a head vase, but I was so surprised to learn that she is also a candle holder. A 1/2-inch candle fits into her neck socket. This versatile piece is copyrighted 1959 and stands 4 inches tall. Although she is not wearing her original earrings, these reproductions are very similar. The original earrings were a little more pointed at their bases. Value: $50-$55.

Santa candle holder—$15-$20; bell—$12-$15; (from Dworkin Collection; photo by Van Blerck Photography).

REMBRANDT SANTA AND SANTA BELL

Rembrandt Santa candle holder with an artist's pallet stands 4 inches tall, and is copyrighted 1960. The other happy Santa with his hands in the air is a bell that stands 5 inches tall and is copyrighted 1958. Value: candle holder—$15-$20; bell—$12-$15.

Carolers trio candle holder: $15-$20 (from Dworkin Collection; photo by Van Blerck Photography).

CAROLERS TRIO CANDLE HOLDER

This Christmas-caroler trio candle holder stands 4-1/2 inches tall and holds a holiday candle on either side. Copyrighted 1959. Value: $15-$20.

Santa candle holders: $30-$35 for set (from Dworkin Collection; photo by Van Blerck Photography).

TRAFFIC-WEARY SANTA CANDLE HOLDERS

These traffic-weary Santas stand 3 inches high and their Christmas autos are 3-1/4 inches long. Sadly enough, they have to obey those traffic light candle rings that are holding up their deliveries. This unique set is copyrighted 1958. Value: $30-$35 for the set.

Reindeer candle holders: $30-$35 for set (from Dworkin Collection; photo by Van Blerck Photography).

REINDEER CANDLE HOLDERS

Reindeer candle holders are beautifully decorated with four brass candle holder antlers. Both pieces stand 5-1/2 inches tall and are numbered 6128L. Value: $30-$35 for the set.

See-saw Santa candle holders: $20-$25 (from Dworkin Collection; photo by Van Blerck Photography).

SEE-SAW SANTA CANDLE HOLDERS

These see-saw Santas are a truly versatile holiday decoration that serves not only as a candle holder, but also a planter or vase for holiday greens or flowers. The planter reads "Greetings" on one side and "Christmas" on the other. These jovial Santas are copyrighted 1960 and have a numeric code of 6384. Value: $20-$25.

Choo-choo Santa candle holders: $25-$30 for set (from Dworkin Collection; photo by Van Blerck Photography).

CHOO-CHOO SANTA CANDLE HOLDERS

Candle holders don't get much cuter than these. Santa pulls the locomotive while an adorable mouse rides for free! Attached with a truly 1950s-era chain is the caboose with a decorated Christmas tree. These fun Christmas train Santas stand 3-1/2 inches and the caboose with Christmas trees are 2-3/4 inches high. Copyrighted 1959. Value: $25-$30 for the set.

Snowmen candelabra: $18-$23 (from Dworkin Collection; photo by Van Blerck Photography).

SNOWMEN CANDELABRA

The snowmen-trio candelabra is 7-3/4 inches long, and the tallest center snowman stands 5 inches tall. It has no copyright date, but it has an "HH" foil sticker. Value: $18-$23.

Santa candelabra—$18-$23; salt & peppers—$12-$18 for set (from Dworkin Collection; photo by Van Blerck Photography).

SANTA CANDELABRA AND SALT & PEPPERS

The Santa-trio candelabra is 8-1/4 inches long, and the tallest center Santa is 5 inches high. This piece has the red and gold Christmas "HH" foil sticker. The salt & peppers are part of the same set. The salt is 2-1/4 inches and the pepper is 2-3/4 inches. These shakers are not signed, but have the "HH" foil sticker. Value: candelabra—$18-$23; salt & peppers—$12-$18 for the set.

Ole' Snowy candle climbers: $35-$45 for pair (from Dworkin Collection; photo by Van Blerck Photography).

OLE' SNOWY CANDLE CLIMBERS

This snowman candle climber is named "Ole' Snowy," and he appeared in Holt-Howard's catalogs not only in ceramic form, but also as a pencil sketch character for the Christmas section of its catalogs. He's too cute for words with his big smile, carrot nose and decorated Christmas tree hat. Ole' Snowy also was issued in candle holders and candle-holder hurricane lamps. Value: $35-$45 for the pair.

Magnet Santa salt & peppers: $35-$45 for each set (from Dworkin Collection; photo by Van Blerck Photography).

MAGNET SANTA SALT & PEPPERS

These magnet salt & pepper Santas have three pouring holes each, so it's hard to determine which one is the salt and which is pepper. But they're so adorable, who cares? Each Santa has a magnet that attaches him either to his gifts or his bag. The Santa on the gifts is stacked 5 inches tall, and the Santa resting on his holiday bag is 3 inches and his bag is 2 inches. Value: $35-

$45 for each set.

Santa candle holders: $20-$25 for the set (from Dworkin Collection; photo by Van Blerck Photography).

SANTA CANDLE HOLDERS

These blue-eyed Santa candle holders stand about 4 inches high. They are signed with the letters "HH" and have a gold and silver rectangular foil sticker. Value: $20-$25 for the set.

Winter Green: candle holder—$12-$18; salt & peppers—$15-$20 for set (from Dworkin Collection; photo by Van Blerck Photography).

WINTER GREEN: NOEL CANDLE HOLDER AND SALT & PEPPERS

Holt-Howard named this series "Winter Green," and this NOEL Candle holder and salt & pepper shakers are but a small portion of this collection. The candle holder, designed to hold 1/2-inch candles, is 8 inches long and 3 inches high. The matching salt & peppers are 4-1/4 inches high and copyrighted 1960. Value: candle holder—$12-$18; salt & peppers—$15-$20 for the set.

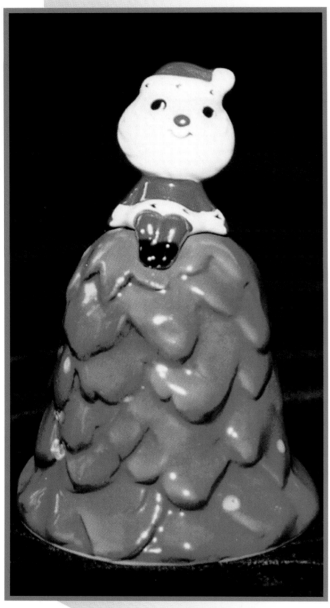

Winter Green: Santa bell—$12-$18 (from collection of and photo by Darline Comisky).

Winter Green: Santa candelabra—$12-$18 (from collection of and photo by Darline Comisky).

WINTER GREEN: SANTA BELL AND CANDELABRA

This bell is also part of the Winter Green collection. Santa sits on top of a holly holiday bell that measures 3-1/2 inches high and 2-1/4 inches wide at the base. Copyrighted 1962. The holly candelabra measures 6 inches high and his copyrighted 1960. Value: $12-$18 each.

Winter Green: ashtrays—$7-$10 for set (from Dworkin Collection; photo by Van Blerck Photography).

Santa letter and pen holder: $35-$45 (from Blair/Rodriguez collection; photo by Mary Norman).

Santa Letter and Pen Holder

Santa has a jingle bell-topped red spiral-coiled cap to hold letters and a red spiral coil at his side to hold a pen. Value: $35-$45.

Elf girl NOEL candle holders: $23-$28 for set (from Dworkin Collection; photo by Van Blerck Photography).

Elf Girl NOEL Candle Holders

This four-piece "NOEL" candle holder set consists of four holly-decorated elves whose bodies spell "NOEL." All four components to this set are 3-1/2 inches high and are copyrighted 1958. Value: $23-$28 for the set.

Winter Green: Ashtrays

These ashtrays are part of Holt-Howard's Winter Green series. This set measures 4-1/2 inches long and is copyrighted 1959. Value: $7-$10 for the set.

Santa cookie/candy jar: $125-$150 (from Dworkin Collection; photo by Van Blerck Photography).

Jolly Holly Mouse candle rings: $35-$45 for set; $65-$75 with original bases (from collection of and photo by Darline Comisky).

JOLLY HOLLY MOUSE CANDLE RINGS/BASES

The "Jolly Holly Mouse" candle rings are 2 inches high and are perched on top of their festive, highly decorated candle holders. This four-piece set is copyrighted 1958. These mice also appear on the Choo-Choo Santa locomotive candle holders (if you look closely, you'll notice them taking a free ride on the rear of the train). Value: $65-$75 for the four-piece set.

Belle Girl Christmas bell: $12-$15 (from Dworkin Collection; photo by Van Blerck Photography).

SANTA COOKIE/CANDY JAR

A Santa cookie and candy jar all in one piece! Santa's hat comes off to store candy, and his head is removable to store cookies. This double-delight jar stands 8-1/2 inches tall and is signed "Holt-Howard, Japan." Value: $125-$150.

BELLE GIRL CHRISTMAS BELL

The 3-inch angel bell is but only one piece of a set of holiday "Jingle" boys and girl "Belles" bells that were designed for a Christmas tree, mantle or table decoration. The bells range from 3 inches to 4 inches. This bell is 3 inches tall and marked #6021. Value: $12-$15.

Santa train planter: $35-$45 (from Dworkin Collection; photo by Van Blerck Photography).

SANTA TRAIN PLANTER

This Santa train planter measures 7-1/2 inches long and 6 inches high. This piece has been restored; however, in its original condition, "Santa Express" is spelled-out in gold letters on the sides of the train. The planter has the "HH" foil sticker. Value: $35-$45.

Santa planter: $30-$35 (from Dworkin Collection; photo by Van Blerck Photography).

SANTA PLANTER

This Santa planter stands 7-1/2 inches tall and has plenty of room in his toy sack behind him to accommodate a nice size plant or floral arrangement. This planter is copyrighted 1961 and numbered 6457. Value: $30-$35.

Doe and fawn planter: $30-$35 (from Dworkin Collection; photo by Van Blerck Photography).

DOE AND FAWN PLANTER

The doe and fawn planter stands 7 inches tall and has an attached planter behind the larger deer for a plant or Christmas greens. Copyrighted 1960. Value: $30-$35.

Santa with bags candle holders: $15-$20 for pair (from Dworkin Collection; photo by Van Blerck Photography).

SANTA WITH BAGS CANDLE HOLDERS

These 3-1/4-inch high Santa-with-gift bag candle holders are copyrighted 1958. Value: $15-$20 for the pair.

Conical Santa salt & peppers: $8-$12 for pair (from Dworkin Collection; photo by Van Blerck Photography).

CONICAL SANTA SALT & PEPPERS

These conical Santa shakers have six pouring holes atop their heads. To tell them apart, one Santa wears a white pompon on his cap for salt, and his companion wears a black pompon for pepper. Both shakers have a gold & silver "HH" foil sticker. Value: $8-$12 for the pair.

Military Santa shakers: $8-$10 each (from Dworkin Collection; photo by Van Blerck Photography).

MILITARY SANTA SHAKERS

These military Santa shakers are not a pair, but a representation of a series of military Santa shakers. One Santa holds a gun, while the other holds a drum. To be correct, both Santas in each set should be holding the same items, either two guns or two drums. These Santas are 3 inches high. Value: $8-$10 each.

Coffee mugs: $15-$20 per set (from Dworkin Collection; photo by Van Blerck Photography).

COFFEE MUGS

Here are two sets of 8-ounce coffee mugs: one set has painted eyes and the other sports green rhinestone eyes. The painted-eye set has a "HH" foil sticker and the rhinestone eyes are signed "Holt-Howard." This Santa mug was introduced by B. Altman & Co., and appeared in its 1958 Christmas catalog. Value: $15-$20 per set of two.

Santa mug with two handles: $12-$18 (from collection of and photo by Darline Comisky).

SANTA MUG WITH TWO HANDLES

This smiling two-handled, handlebar-mustache Santa mug is 2-3/4 inches tall and 4 inches wide. Copyrighted 1963. Value: $12-$18.

Christmas snow babies salt & peppers: $25-$30 for set (from collection of and photo by Marlene Krumm Sanders).

CHRISTMAS SNOW BABIES SALT & PEPPERS

Copyrighted 1959, these Christmas snow babies salt & peppers are about 3 inches high. Value: $25-$30 for the set.

Christmas snow babies candy holders: $5-$8 each (from Dworkin Collection; photo by Van Blerck Photography).

CHRISTMAS SNOW BABIES CANDY HOLDERS

Christmas snow babies climbing up on Santa's boots are slightly more than 2 inches high, copyrighted 1959 and numbered 6109. Santa's boots probably were used to hold Christmas candy, and it appears that's what these little guys are looking for! Value: $5-$8 each.

Miniature ornaments: $15-$20 for set (from Dworkin Collection; photo by Van Blerck Photography).

MINIATURE ORNAMENTS

These miniature Christmas ornaments were packed eight to the box. Each piece has a blue and white paper sticker that reads "Japan" or "Made in Japan." The candy cane-striped gift box that they were sold in has the "HH" foil sticker. All the pieces have gold-colored string to hang them on a Christmas tree, and the figures range in size from 1 inch to 1-1/2 inches. Truly a miniature holiday delight! Value: $15-$20 for set of eight.

Holly girls salt and peppers: $15-$20 for set (from Dworkin Collection; photo by Van Blerck Photography).

HOLLY GIRLS SALT & PEPPERS

The salt and peppers holly girls hold up large poinsettias designating a "S" or "P" to identify their shaker's contents. This festive duo is 4 inches high, both are numbered 6216 and have an "HH" foil sticker. Value: $15-$20 for the set.

Ermine Angels: salt & peppers—$20-$25 for set (from Dworkin Collection; photo by Van Blerck Photography).

ERMINE ANGELS: SALT & PEPPERS

Holt-Howard designed a series of Christmas angels it named "Ermine Angels." All the pieces to this set were created as pairs and always came as a set of two. One angel would hold a pair of red holiday bells, while her sister angel always wore a muff. All these cute bisque-faced angels were highly decorated with ermine trim around their heads and dresses. Holt-Howard called this trim ermine; today, collectors refer to it as "spaghetti art," since all the trim is made up of tiny spaghetti-like ceramic pieces. Ermine angel shakers stand 3-3/4 inches tall and are signed with the letters "HH" accompanied with an "HH" foil sticker. Value: $20-$25 for the set.

Ermine Angels: candle holders—$25-$35 complete set (from collection of and photo by Darline Comisky).

ERMINE ANGELS: CANDLE HOLDERS/RINGS

Ermine Angel candle holders are 4-1/4 inches tall and have their attached candle holder bases located behind them. Each candle holder, copyrighted 1958,

originally came with its own snowflake candle ring which slides over the candle. These snowflake candle rings match the snowflakes on the Ermine Angel planters (pictured below). Value: $25-$35 for complete four-piece set.

Ermine Angel: planter—$25-$30 (from Dworkin Collection; photo by Van Blerck Photography).

Ermine Angel: planter—$25-$30 (from Dworkin Collection; photo by Van Blerck Photography).

ERMINE ANGELS: PLANTERS

These planters measure 3-1/2 inches long and 4 inches high. The front of the planters are decorated with three large snowflakes. Both are copyrighted 1958. Value: $25-$30 each.

SANTA KINGS

Holt-Howard's Santa Kings series is a real eye-catcher. All of these pieces are highly decorated with gold and are very festive for the holidays. These two santas are very unique.

Santa King: smoking sets—$30-$35 each set (from Dworkin Collection; photo by Van Blerck Photography).

SANTA KING: SMOKING SETS

These two Santas are very unique. The shorter 4-inch Santa's crown comes off and is believed to serve as an astray, while his base holds cigarettes. His 5-inch companion piece's crown is also removable (it might be a storage container for matches). Both pieces are copyrighted 1960. There is a set of four very small crown ashtrays which are part of this set. Value: $30-$35 for each set.

Santa King: candle holders—$80-$90 for set (from Blair/Rodriguez collection; photo by Mary Norman).

SANTA KING: CANDLE HOLDERS

This pair of Santa kings candle holders is 4-3/4 inches tall. Each has a 1-inch opening in the center of Santa's crown to accommodate a large candle. Copyrighted 1960. Value: $80-$90 for the set.

Santa King: candle holder/vase—$40-$45 (from Dworkin Collection; photo by Van Blerck Photography).

SANTA KING: CANDLE HOLDER/VASE

This 5-inch Santa is believed to be a combination candle holder/vase. He has two small red candle holders with 1/2-inch openings as part of the design of his crown. There are also three holes in the center of his head to insert live Christmas greens in his crown. Copyrighted 1960. Value: $40-$45.

Santa King: decanter and glasses—$85-$95 for set (from Blair/Rodriguez collection; photo by Mary Norman).

SANTA KING: DECANTER AND GLASSES

This Santa King liquor set includes a decanter with four matching crown-shaped shot glasses. Value: $85-$95 for complete five-piece set.

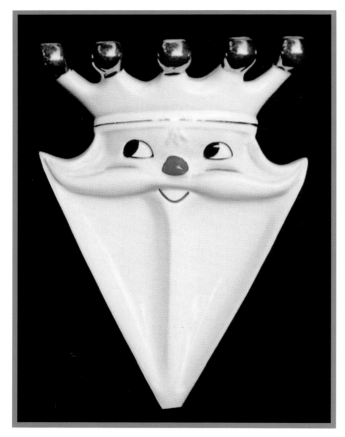

Santa King: tray—$35-$45 (from collection of and photo by Darline Comisky).

SANTA KING: TRAY

A wonderful party server for the holidays! This Santa king divided tray is 9 inches long and 6-1/2 inches wide to hold lots of holiday goodies. The Santa dish is copyrighted 1960. Value: $35-$45.

Wee Three Kings: candle holders—$45-$55 for set (from Dworkin Collection; photo by Van Blerck Photography).

WEE THREE KINGS: CANDLE HOLDERS

This trio of candle holders was named "Wee Three Kings" by Holt-Howard and have 1-inch openings in their crowns to hold a large candle. These three wise guys are 4-1/2 inches tall and copyrighted 1960. Value: $45-$55 for the complete three-piece set.

Wee Three Kings: bells/candle holders—$45-$55 for set (from Dworkin Collection; photo by Van Blerck Photography).

WEE THREE KINGS: BELLS/CANDLE HOLDERS

A different version of the Wee Three Kings theme, these guys are smaller, measuring only 3-1/2 inches and are combination bell/candle holders. Each has a bell clangor inside its base. Their crowns are only in the front and do not go completely around their heads. These items have only 1/2-inch openings in their crowns and they hold much smaller candles than their larger brothers. This dual-functional three-piece set is copyrighted 1960. Value: $45-$55 for the complete three-piece set.

Naughty choir boys candle holders: $20-$25 for set (from collection of and photo by Darline Comisky).

NAUGHTY CHOIR BOYS CANDLE HOLDERS

The naughty choir boys candle holders are unique: one boy has a sling shot and the other has a gun in holster (plus a black eye). Value: $20-$25 for the set.

Camel candle holders: $25-$35 for pair (from Dworkin Collection; photo by Van Blerck Photography).

CAMEL CANDLE HOLDERS

Highly decorated camel candle holders are adorned with jewel-like metallic foil and beads on top of their heads. Each camel is 4 inches long, and 3-1/2 inches high. Both have 1-inch openings on their backs to accommodate large candles. This set is copyrighted 1960 and numbered 6416. Value: $25-$35 for the pair.

Camel planter: $30-$35 (from collection of and photo by Darline Comisky).

CAMEL PLANTER

This camel planter is part of the camel candle holders set and is 6-1/2 inches long and 4-1/2 inches high. This planter is copyrighted 1961 and numbered 6417. Value: $30-$35.

Red angel candle holders: $12-$18 for pair (from Connie and Jeff Knecht Collection; photo by Jeff Knecht).

RED ANGEL CANDLE HOLDERS

These twin Christmas angels are candle holders that measure 4-1/2 inches high. They are signed and copyrighted 1961. Value: $12-$18 for the pair.

Totem-pole Santa candle holders: $15-$20 each (from collection of and photo by Darline Comisky).

TOTEM-POLE SANTA CANDLE HOLDERS

Totem-pole Santa candle holders stacked up to 8-1/2 inches in adorable Holt-Howard style. Each Santa extends his arms to hold a candle. Copyrighted 1958. Value: $15-$20 each.

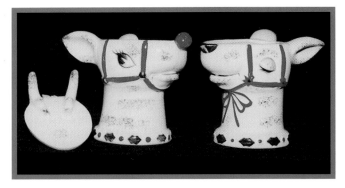

Reindeer creamer & sugar: $35-$40 for set (from collection of and photo by Darline Comisky).

REINDEER CREAMER & SUGAR

A loving reindeer couple decked out in holiday trim comprise this cute sugar & creamer set. The sugar has an antler lid and stands 3-1/2 inches, while his creamer mate stands 2-1/4 inches. Both are numbered 6182. Value: $35-$40 for the set.

Girl Christmas tree air freshener: $18-$23 (from Blair/Rodriguez collection; photo by Mary Norman).

GIRL CHRISTMAS TREE AIR FRESHENER

Girl Christmas tree air freshener stands 6-1/2 inches tall and is copyrighted 1959. This pretty miss holds wicks to sweeten the air. A great piece to fragrance your home with the scent of pine or spruce for the holidays. Value: $18-$23.

Santa and reindeer planter: $25-$35 (from Blair/Rodriguez collection; photo by Mary Norman).

SANTA AND REINDEER PLANTER

Santa holds the reins while his planter sleigh is being pulled by his two candle-holder reindeer. Value: $25-$35.

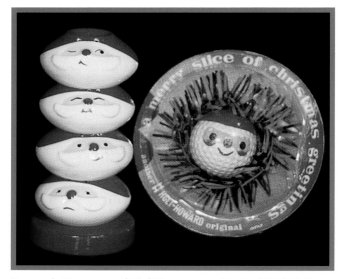

Santa salt & peppers—$18-$23 per set; golf ball—$12-$15 (from Blair/Rodriguez collection; photo by Mary Norman).

SANTAS SALT & PEPPERS AND GOLF BALL

Two sets of stackable Santa salt & peppers sit neatly in totem-pole fashion on top of their red, wooden storage rack. Both the shakers and the storage rack have the "HH" foil stickers. Also pictured is an original Holt-Howard Santa golf ball in its original packaging. Value: salt & peppers—$18-$23 per set; golf ball—$12-$15 in original wrap.

Candle holders: Madonna and child—$20-$25; children praying— $15-$20 each (from Dworkin Collection; photo by Van Blerck Photography).

Santa wall pocket: $30-$35 (from Blair/Rodriguez collection; photo by Mary Norman).

RELIGIOUS CANDLE HOLDERS

Holt-Howard produced many religious ceramics to celebrate Christmas. The Madonna and child candle holder holds two large candles and is copyrighted 1959. The others, the set of two children, are praying in what Holt-Howard called "shadow boxes." Each is 4 inches high and holds two large candles. Both pieces are copyrighted 1960. Value: Madonna and child—$20-$25; children praying—$15-$20 each.

Angel candle holders and rings: $30-$35 for set (from Dworkin Collection; photo by Van Blerck Photography).

SANTA WALL POCKET

Santa holds a gift while standing on what appears to be a beautiful Christmas ornament; it is, in reality, a wall pocket designed to hold Christmas greens or a plant. Value: $30-$35.

ANGEL CANDLE HOLDERS AND RINGS

Two angel-brothers candle holders are tending to ringing their candle ring bells. The pair is copyrighted 1960. The bigger brother stands 4 inches tall and the little brother is 3-1/2 inches tall. Value: $30-$35 for the four-piece set.

Angel/Baby Jesus candle holders: $18-$23 for pair (from Dworkin Collection; photo by Van Blerck Photography).

ANGEL/BABY JESUS CANDLE HOLDERS

Guitar-playing angels and the Baby Jesus stand 4 inches high and hold one large candle each. This set is copyrighted 1963. Value: $18-$23 for the pair.

Angel candle holders: $15-$20 for pair (from Dworkin Collection; photo by Van Blerck Photography).

ANGEL CANDLE HOLDERS

This guitar and violin playing "Angel Duet" candle holders are 7-1/2 inches long, and 4-1/2 inches high. Although the copyright date is not clear, it appears to read 1960. Value: $15-$20 for the pair.

Santa salt & peppers: $12-$15 for set (from Dworkin Collection; photo by Van Blerck Photography).

SANTA SALT & PEPPERS

Although these salt & peppers look like papermache, they are low-glazed ceramic pieces. The Santas stand 4-1/2 inches tall and were made much later than all of the collectibles in this book—about 1972. Value: $12-$15 for the set.

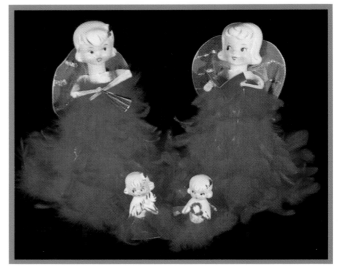

Feathered angels: large—$10-$12 each; small—$4-$6 each (from Blair/Rodriguez collection; photo by Mary Norman).

FEATHERED ANGELS

Although these pieces are not 100% ceramic, their faces are. They represent an era in Christmas collectibles that is gone forever. The larger feathered angels stand 8 inches and were sold as a set of three to the box. The angels stare to their left and each holds something different. The two larger angels are pictured with two, 3-inch angel party favors. The angel party favors were possibly only issued in red or white. The larger angels were issued in white, green, pink and red feathers. Value: large—$10-$12 each; small—$4-$6 each.

Feathered angel harp player: $10-$12 (from Dworkin Collection; photo by Van Blerck Photography).

FEATHERED ANGEL HARP PLAYER

Here's the third musician member of our set of three large angels. Although these angels are not signed, they all have the red and gold "HH" foil sticker on their bases. Value: $10-$12.

Feathered angels: large—$10-$12 each; small—$4-$6 each (from Dworkin Collection; photo by Van Blerck Photography).

FEATHERED ANGELS

Here are two more musically inclined feathered angels in pink-feather gowns, accompanied by another party favor angel in white (holding a candy cane in her hands). Value: large—$10-$12; small—$4-$6.

Christmas twins: $8-$12 each (from Dworkin Collection; photo by Van Blerck Photography).

CHRISTMAS TWINS

The Christmas twins have paper and foil outfits, but also have ceramic faces. These twins stare at each other and stand 6-1/4 inches tall. Value: $8-$12 each.

Santa music box/candle holder: $35-$45 (from Connie and Jeff Knecht Collection; photo by Jeff Knecht).

SANTA MUSIC BOX/CANDLE HOLDER

The Winking Santa music box stands 10-1/2 inches tall. As the music box plays, Santa turns to the tune of "Jingle Bells." This piece has an "HH" foil sticker, is copyrighted 1960 and is numbered 6042. Value: $35-$45.

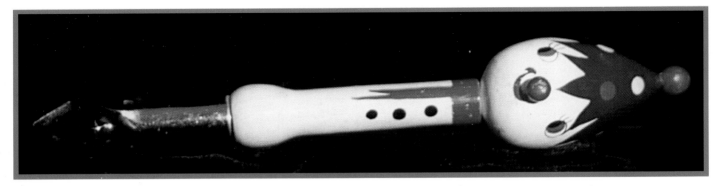

Snowman bottle opener: $18-$23 (from Blair/Rodriguez Collection; photo by Mary Norman).

SNOWMAN BOTTLE OPENER

This cute snowman bottle opener is all smiles and adorned with a Christmas tree hat. He is made of wood and stainless steel. Value: $18-$23.

Christmas tree candle holder: $20-$30 (from collection of and photo by Darline Comisky).

CHRISTMAS TREE CANDLE HOLDER

This ceramic Christmas tree candle holder is curved in the back and bowed in the front. Copyrighted 1958, it comes with all the trim and holds six candles. It stands 6-1/2 inches tall and is 4-3/4 inches wide. Value: $20-$30.